design centre
LONDON

THE HOME OF THE WORLD'S GREATEST DESIGN AND DECORATION BRANDS

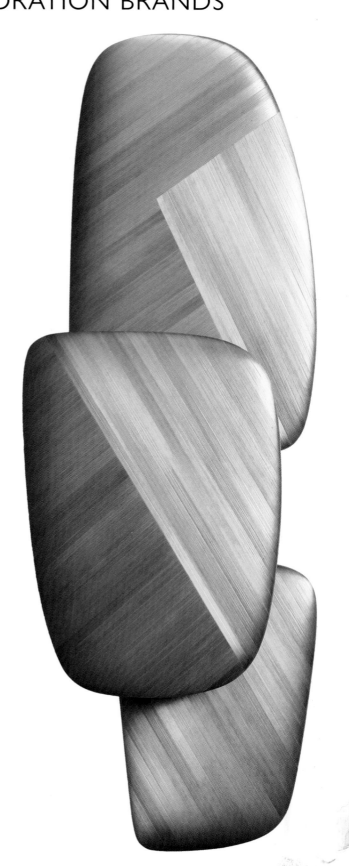

130+ SHOWROOMS

OVER 600 INTERNATIONAL BRANDS

ONE ADDRESS

....

SAVE THE DATE

WOW!HOUSE
3 JUNE – 3 JULY

FOCUS/25
15 – 19 SEPTEMBER

FOCUS/25:
THE LONGER VIEW
22 SEPTEMBER – 16 OCTOBER

....

Design Centre, Chelsea Harbour
London SW10 0XE
+44 (0)20 7225 9166

www.dcch.co.uk

May 2025

COVER PHOTOGRAPH WILLIAM JESS LAIRD

Gardens

Kitchens & Bathrooms

Lifestyle

Regulars

TO SUBSCRIBE

Subscribe for six issues for just £6 – visit homesandgardenssubs.com/MAY25

DIGITAL EDITIONS AND PAST ISSUES

These can be downloaded at homesandgardenssubs.com/digital or order print editions at homesandgardenssubs.com/backissue

HOMES & GARDENS

Global Brand Director and Group Editor in Chief Sarah Spiteri
Editor (Print) Jo Bailey
Editor (Digital) Jennifer Ebert
Creative Director Emma Williams
Art Editor Meredith Davies
Group Chief Sub-Editor/Production Editor Jennifer Spaeth
Managing Editor Zara Stacey

Editorial Assistant Holly Ransome
Contributing Houses Editor Vivienne Ayers

Head of Interiors Hebe Hatton
UK Content Editor Sophia Pouget
Content Editors, Interiors Charlotte Olby and Molly Malsom
News Writers, Interiors Abby Wilson and Eleanor Richardson
Sleep Editor Emilia Hitching
Kitchen Appliances Editor Lydia Hayman

Head of Celebrity Style Megan Slack
News Writers, Celebrity Style Hannah Ziegler and Sophie Edwards

Head of Gardens Rachel Bull
Head of E-Commerce Alex David
Content Editors, Gardens Drew Swainston and Thom Rutter
News Writer, Gardens Tenielle Jordison

Head of Solved Punteha van Terheyden
Content Editor, Solved Chiana Dickson
News Writer, Solved Ottilie Blackhall
Home Tech Editor Dan Fauzi

Social Media Editor Anna Aylward
Assistant Social Media Editor Anna Herring
Newsletter Editor Vivian Cheng

Magazine Contributors Amelia Thorpe, Amy Moorea Wong, Arabella Youens, Emma J Page, Jacky Hobbs, Jessica Salter, Kate Worthington, Kiera Buckley-Jones, Laura Vinden, Linda Clayton, Pippa Blenkinsop, Roddy Clarke, Rory Robertson and Zia Allaway

Managing Director Jason Orme
Content Director (Audience) Lucy Searle
Content Director (Social) Francesca York
Content Director (E-Commerce) Lindsey Davis

FUTURE Connectors. Creators. Experience Makers.

Future plc is a public company quoted on the London Stock Exchange (symbol: FUTR) www.futureplc.com

Chief Executive Officer **Kevin Li Ying**
Non-Executive Chairman **Richard Huntingford**
Chief Financial Officer **Sharjeel Suleman**

Tel +44 (0)1225 442 244

ipso. Regulated

recycle

SUBSCRIPTIONS
Online orders: www.magazinesdirect.com/XHG
Email help@magazinesdirect.com

Homes & Gardens (ISSN 0018-4233 USPS 7458) is published 12 times a year by Future Publishing Limited, Quay House, The Ambury, Bath BA1 1UA. One-year full subscription rates for 12 issues including postage & packing: UK £69; Europe €141; Rest of world £155.88. For subscription enquiries please email help@magazinesdirect.com. The US annual subscription price is $160. Airfreight and mailing in the USA by agent named World Container INC 150-15, 183rd St, Jamaica, NY 11413, USA. Periodicals Postage Paid at Brooklyn, NY 11256. Subscription records are maintained at Future Publishing Limited, 121-141 Westbourne Terrace, London W2 6JR. Air Business Ltd. is acting as our mailing agent. All prices include postage and packaging. POSTMASTER: Send address changes to: Homes & Gardens, Air Business Ltd, c/o World Container INC 150-15, 183rd St, Jamaica, NY 11413, USA.

Manage your subscription online with MyMagazine. Visit www.mymagazine.co.uk/FAQ to view frequently asked questions or log in at www.mymagazine.co.uk

Commercial Director Clare Chamberlain
Commercial Director Glenn Iceton
Ad Director Victoria Vatistas
Business Director Marina Connolly
International and Luxury Account Director Carole Bunce
Account Manager Rosie Radford
Head of Project Management Abi Dougherty
Insert Sales – Canopy Media Paloma Walder

Group Art Director Alison Walter
Group Production Editor Maxine Clarke
Chief Sub-Editor Carly Rigley
Senior Sub-Editors Marian McNamara and Karen Wiley
Art Production Director Nicola Tillman
Art Production Designers Chris Saggers and Phil Dunk
Group Production Manager Stephen Catherall
Production Manager Bill Argent
Senior Ad Production Manager Jo Crosby
Advertisement Copy and Make-up Barry Skinner

Head of Brand Partnerships (Licensing) David Abbott
Partner Manager Syndication Efi Mandrides
Head of Print Licensing Rachel Shaw

Trade Marketing Manager Henry Smith
VP Marketforce & Subscription Operations Joel Griffiths

EDITORIAL ENQUIRIES homesandgardens@futurenet.com
Homes & Gardens, Future, 121-141 Westbourne Terrace, London W2 6JR
All colleagues are contactable at firstname.lastname@futurenet.com

Printed by Walstead UK Limited
Distributed by Marketforce (UK) Ltd, 121-141 Westbourne Terrace,
London W2 6JR, mfcommunications@futurenet.com
Homes & Gardens is available for licensing. To find our more
contact licensing@futurenet.com and view available content
at www.futurecontenthub.com
ISSN 0018-4233

Paolo Moschino

PRESENTS

THE WOVEN COLLECTION

EDITOR'S PICK

Sally Denning of Blackshore Style – and the stylist behind many of our photo shoots – has designed a stunning rug collection with Tate & Darby - I love this design.

A

s we worked on the May issue, the *Homes & Gardens* team became eager to embrace the outdoors, tackle gardening projects and plan that dream getaway. At this time of year, the focus naturally shifts from interiors to exteriors and we begin to think about how the garden can extend the home. Our edit of gorgeous outdoor furniture (page 145) will help you do just that and the decorating feature (page 44) highlights the latest outdoor textiles, which have evolved from stiff and uncomfortable to soft and luxurious – so versatile, they can be enjoyed both indoors and out. Although unpredictable UK weather can make this challenging, I always seize the chance to fling open the back doors and dine alfresco. While my home may not be set against Mallorca's Tramuntana mountains like the breathtaking garden featured this month (page 128), designed by Mashamba Garden Design, my husband and I have adopted similar zoning principles, creating distinct areas for different activities. I love how design can inspire, regardless of its location or origin. Our cover story, a beautiful Tuscan farmhouse by the always-impeccable Nicola Harding (page 76), embodies this idea perfectly. While set in Italy, its soulful design and use of colour can translate to any home. Similarly, Guy Goodfellow's project (page 88), although in Shropshire, features a courtyard with Mediterranean charm, thanks to its pediment and multiple columns. I hope this issues leaves you feeling inspired.

Jo Bailey, Editor

NEWSLETTER

Scan this QR code to enjoy *Homes & Gardens* in your inbox with our email newsletter

SUBSCRIBE TODAY

Don't miss our introductory subscription offer – 6 issues for £6. Turn to page 118 for details.

FOLLOW US ON

INSTAGRAM @homesandgardensofficial
X @homesandgardens
FACEBOOK @homesandgardens
PINTEREST @homesgardensuk
TIKTOK @homesandgardensofficial
WHATSAPP Homes & Gardens

PHOTOGRAPHS (EDITOR'S PICK) TOLLGARD; (TOP) FABRIC IN BACKGROUND JAYSHREE EMBROIDERED PEACOCK REPEAT IN GREY/RUSSET, £OFANY

Fresh designs,
timeless surfaces

MANDARIN STONE

NATURAL STONE | PORCELAIN | DECORATIVE TILES

16 INSPIRATIONAL UK SHOWROOMS

mandarinstone.com

OBJECTS OF
desire

Pretty pieces that have caught our editor's eye

1. The Greenwich camelback sofa, from £8,400 excluding fabric, Lorfords Contemporary
2. Mafalda fabric, £120m, Claire de Quénetain at August+Co
3. Ere loop hook in brass, £161, Unearthen at Petra
4. Caspian chest of drawers in Sanguine Red Oak High Gloss No Grain, from £2,800, Isabel & Co
5. Small scallop shell wall light in Capri, £1,674, Porta Romana
6. Spigolatura No. 62 woven artwork, £2,500, Susanna Costantini →

Little Greene®
— PAINT & PAPER —

FINE PAINTS & PAPERS
IN ASSOCIATION WITH

National Trust

Bring your interiors to life with 'Storybook Papers.'

A whimsical new wallpaper collection for children and grown-ups alike.

Order your complimentary colourcard, or find your nearest stockist at littlegreene.com
Colour Consultancy service available nationwide and online

littlegreene.com

1. Mill Oak wallpaper in Viridis, £159 a roll, Fanny Shorter
2. Rattan urn in Green, from £35, Charles Orchard
3. Rattan flush ceiling light, £130, Nina Campbell x Next
4. Anemone handmade tile, £115, Edith Morris for The Shop Floor Project
5. Welcome round dining table in Caramel, £16,825, Matthew Raw at The New Craftmaker
6. Bayleaf floating bedside table, £1,900, Sebastian Cox
7. The Scavo lamp, from £2,500, Studio Valerie Name →

1. Campo dei Fiori fabric, £630 per piece (68x90cm), Dedar
2. Pause chair in polished steel and natural oak in Celeste velvet no. 23, price on request, Timothée Mion for La Chance
3. Plessey mirror, from £6,663, Novocastrian
4. Dazzleships Monochrome Gold Top ceramic artwork, £840, Eddie Knevett at Ruup & Form
5. Cloud sofa, £14,950, Tom Faulkner
6. Tradition 01 flatweave rug in Orange, from £245, Nordic Knots
7. Spiral coasters, £60.16 for a set of four, Sophie Lou Jacobsen →

CORAGGIO

European luxury since 1979

Unit 001 Worlds Ends Studio, 132-134 Lots Road, London SW10ORJ

Elevato wallcovering.

matki

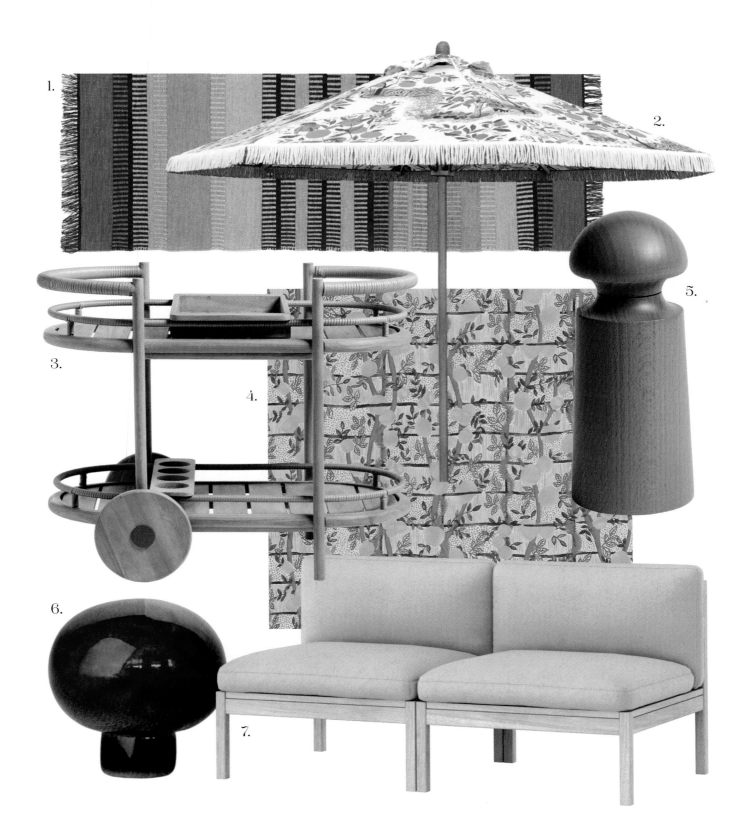

1. Muturi indoor/outdoor rug, £275, Designers Guild
2. Josef Frank Citrus Garden parasol, from £4,565, Plia Parasols
3. Raymond drinks trolley, £1,295, Oka
4. Garden Party fabric, £168m, Gert Voorjans for Jim Thompson
5. Salt/pepper mill in Green, from £44, David Mellor
6. Blue ceramic knob with ceramic pillar, from £36, Byron & Gómez
7. Modular two-seater sofa in Field 463, £2,310, Moebe at Twentytwentyone →

1. The Long Elowen chandelier, £18,500, Studio Peake
2. Jayshree embroidered fabric in Spice/Russet, £256m, Zoffany
3. Perry mirror, from £598, Anthropologie
4. The Alexis bench in Jajim Stripe in Chestnut, £5,400, Soane Britain
5. Embroidered Lark cushion cover, £85, Toast
6. Kitty chair, £8,160, Jamb
7. Trefoil wall bracket, from £612, Sibyl Colefax & John Fowler

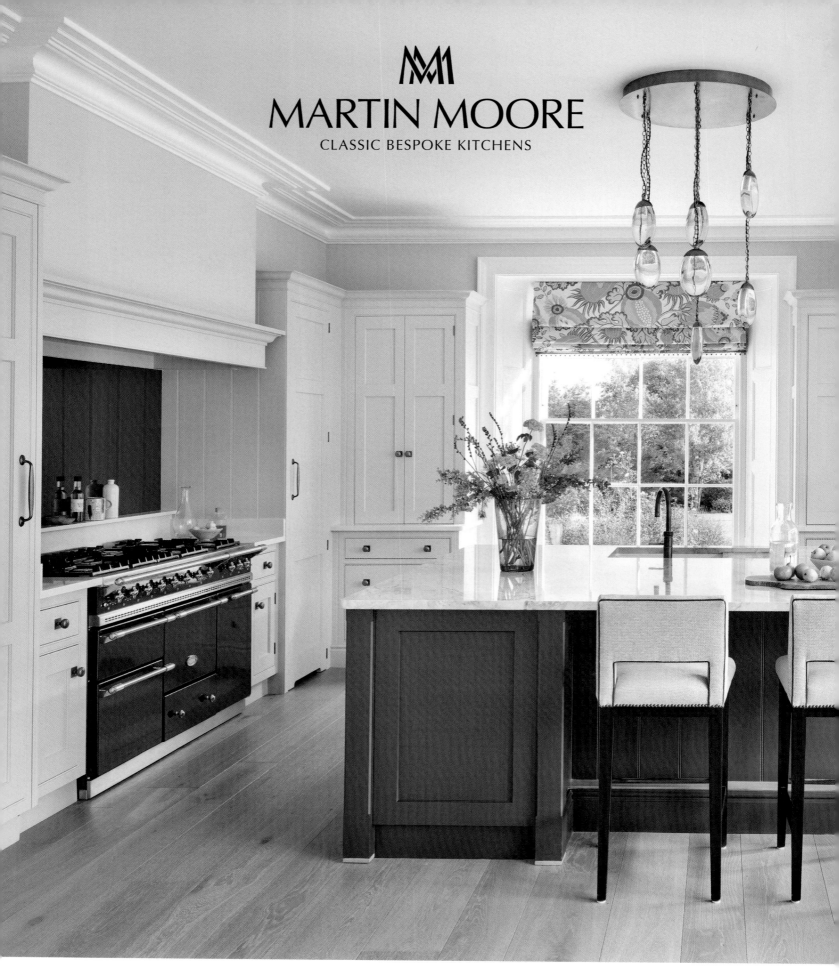

MARTIN MOORE
CLASSIC BESPOKE KITCHENS

The May Edit

A CURATION OF THE BEST DESIGN AND HOME IDEAS

FEATURE LAURA VINDEN
PHOTOGRAPH JOSHUA LAWRENCE

CRAFT PROJECT
Makers Made is a curated online gallery founded by five artists –
Hal Haines, Harlie Brown, Kate Sellers, Rosie Harbottle and Sophie
Harpley. The platform showcases original, handmade homeware, from
ceramics and furniture to lighting and textiles, connecting buyers with
artisans. By supporting independent UK-based makers, Makers Made
fosters a community where artistry and craftsmanship thrive, providing
customers with distinctive pieces to enrich their homes. →

&

All the latest interiors news, including a
focus on tiled floors, the design show
to visit and the people and brands
supporting UK makers

BRONZED BEAUTY

Audo Copenhagen's Pavot collection, designed with New York aesthete Colin King, features three vessels inspired by poppy seed heads. Cast in aluminium with a brown-bronzed patina, the centrepiece (shown), £245; bowl, £140, and vase, £155, showcase elongated silhouettes, soft curves and a subtly footed base for a refined, tactile look.

Romantic textures

From Ralph Lauren Home comes the Rue Bohème fabric collection, capturing Parisian bohemian glamour with a romantic, artistic aesthetic. It features distressed florals, classic ticking stripes and heirloom embroideries in shades of indigo, chambray, cream and white. True to Ralph Lauren's style, rich textures – denim, rugged canvas, paint-splattered velvet and linen with metallic touches – add depth and interest. Highlights include Impasto Floral, £55m, and Beaton Floral, £60m, embodying a time-worn feel that enhances the collection's charming sensibilities.

Weaving stories

Pelican House and Lucy Williams Home introduce Havens, a three-piece rug collection inspired by landscapes close to Lucy's heart – England, Wales and Greece. Acres captures English folk-art charm with naive floral and animal motifs. Dunes, woven from jute, reflects the Welsh coast with patterns inspired by Welsh blankets. Nisi, made in New Zealand wool, features Greek key and fish motifs. Handmade in India, the collection starts at £1,156 and is available in two sizes, with custom options.

LAYERED FINISH

Julian Chichester introduces Monterey, a capsule collection created in collaboration with architectural design studio Bernard London. The collection – featuring a bedside table, chest of drawers, console and cabinet (shown), £3,550 – is available in Brighton White or lacquer, with brass inlay details and faux cork.

Switched on

The Soho Lighting Company has announced a collaboration with Historic Royal Palaces, drawing inspiration from sites such as Kensington Palace and Hampton Court Palace. The Royal Palace Collection reflects the history and character of these landmarks through beautifully designed switches, from £69.

PHOTOGRAPHS (GABLED GRANDEUR)
PAUL WHITBREAD

GABLED GRANDEUR

Berdoulat, renowned for its restoration of historic buildings and timeless furniture, introduces the Gable four-poster bed. True to its name, the headboard echoes the gabled rooftops of Amsterdam's canal houses and strikes a balance between grandeur and understated elegance. Made from walnut and priced at £8,628, it is available in standard and bespoke sizes.

Meet the maker

Founded by Shweta Mistry, Mistry Designs creates heritage-led fabrics and wallpapers, blending rare pigments, traditional techniques and digital innovation. Can you tell us about your background?
I grew up appreciating arts and crafts in design and the power of making/creating, seeing my father cherishing a grain of wood, himself being in the furniture business and seeing craftspeople in his workshop. The importance of arts and crafts has been imbibed in me and gravitated me towards fine arts as a starting point. It all began while I was studying Master of Research in Creative Practices at Glasgow School of Art, having previous degrees in Fine Art and Creative Painting along with a Summer Programme with Rhode Island School of Design. Therefore, my background creates a world view, with an affinity and appreciation for the arts and crafts in design.
Where do you look for inspiration? Inspiration is everywhere. Walking in nature, going to museums and galleries, heritage arts and crafts, history, which are all evident in the designs we create at Mistry Designs.
What is it you love most about what you do? I am very thankful and privileged to love what I do. Preservation of traditional arts and crafts in our ever-changing modern world is a vital means of providing the timeless values that bring stability to human life. My mission is to invigorate forgotten arts for future generations through our created designs.
If you weren't a textile designer, what was your plan B?
My plan B would be in line with my plan A, which is to bring the heritage arts and crafts in new light for the next generations. In fact, there is no plan B, I truly believe in plan A. →

On the move

Portable lighting has never been more refined than the Copper Coast rechargeable accent light by Visual Comfort & Co. Priced at £1,999, it is available in three finishes, including Polished Brass (shown), and made in collaboration with Ireland's Waterford Crystal, taking inspiration from County Waterford's dramatic coastline.

London Craft Week

Returning for its 11th edition from 12–18 May, London Craft Week will present over 400 exhibitions, masterclasses and workshops, celebrating craft across the capital for all ages. Secret Ceramics (below) at Christie's is a charitable initiative showcasing over 100 works by renowned and emerging artists. Proceeds will fund four youth ceramics studios, allowing young people from disadvantaged backgrounds to explore clay. At Frieze No. 9 Cork Street, there will be a group showcase from Béton Brut, featuring works by Grace Prince, as well as David Horan's 'vegan vellum' pieces (top right). Meanwhile, Cromwell Place will spotlight artisans from South Korea, Myanmar and Japan. Highlights will include Soluna Art Group's exhibition of work crafted from horsehair, ceramics, metal and glass by Dahye Jeong (above); and Turquoise Mountain (top left) will display examples of traditional Burmese artisanal lacquerware, silk weaving and goldsmithing.

Regency revival

Luke Edward Hall, the celebrated British artist and designer, brings his signature romanticism and love of history to his collaboration with The Lacquer Company. Inspired by Regency-era painted furniture, the Benedict chest of drawers, £4,995, is a striking trompe l'oeil piece in four colourways, showcasing Luke's flair for storytelling through design. Crafted using Vietnam's finest Son Mai lacquer, each chest is handmade using time-honoured techniques, resulting in a richly layered and luminous finish. →

Ledbury
STUDIO

KITCHENS by CHARLIE SMALLBONE

4b Ledbury Mews North London W11 2AF
020 7566 6794
ledburystudio.com

PHOTOGRAPHS (ORGANIC FORMS) ALUN CALLENDER,
COURTESY THE ARTIST AND HIGNELL GALLERY

Heritage hues

At the end of this month, paint maker Graphenstone will launch The Colour Collection – a palette of 120 shades, including 24 new hues created in collaboration with English Heritage, inspired by the historic properties it helps preserve. The mineral-based paints, from £27.50 for 1ltr, are breathable and durable, making them ideal for old buildings. Shades such as Entrance Hall Blue and Kenwood Cream (shown), inspired by Kenwood House, blend traditional materials like lime with graphene – one of the world's strongest carbon fibres. Delving into the English Heritage archives, the collection draws on wallpapers, fabrics and historic paint documents to honour the elegance of period properties while offering resilience for modern living.

À TABLE

The Jardins Sculptés collection by Gilles et Boissier, in collaboration with Bourg-Joly Malicorne, one of France's oldest faience houses, brings the beauty of the natural world to the table. Crafted in earthenware, each piece – servers and dishes from €190 – draws inspiration from vine leaves, squash and fish.

OPEN FOR BUSINESS

British furniture maker Ercol celebrates a landmark moment with the opening of its first-ever stand-alone store. Located in the heart of London's design district, the flagship on the King's Road presents the complete Ercol collection, from mid-century icons to modern classics. Customers can personalise timeless designs such as the Heritage love seat (shown), from £999.

Organic forms

Into Being is a new exhibition by artist Laura Ellen Bacon at Yorkshire Sculpture Park's 18th-century Chapel, from 5 April to 7 September. Made from sustainable Somerset willow, the installation's sinuous curves weave around the building, evoking cocoons, burrows and seed pods. Extending six metres into the nave and three metres up the wall, the display allows visitors to step inside to experience shifting light and shadow. After the exhibition, the willow will be used to create wildlife habitats.

A light touch

Delightful glass designs that will sparkle in the sun

(Clockwise, from top left) Marea large glass **pendant** in warm hues, £5,514, Ochre. Lara **candleholder**, £42, Byon at Nordic Nest. Red Classic Poppy **flower**, £80, Sandralexandra. Pink and white swirl **wine glass**, £195 for a pair, Henry Holland Studio. Miami **wine cooler**, £620, Gather. Glass **cylinders**, £1,430 each, Edmond Byrne at Flow Gallery. Donut **side table**, £965, Deya ⊡

FEATURE HOLLY RANSOME **PHOTOGRAPHS** (GLASS CYLINDERS) ISOBEL NAPIER

In detail: floor tiles

What's new and noteworthy for this stylish underfoot surface

Precision in every piece

If you're after floor tiling that makes an impact, it's worth perusing the new Composition collection from tile and stone specialists Lapicida. The recently launched 12 designs formed of impressive collages of cut stone feature abstracted patterns, including checks and argyle print, signifying a new modern design direction for the stone experts. Yet rest assured that quality remains top-grade – the designs are made from a mix of premium natural stones, such as travertine, marble and basalt. The beauty of the stones' organic colours and markings shine through, and the collection's palette is defined by sophisticated natural hues such as amber browns, jade greens, monochromes and sandy beiges. The Composition collection works on walls as well as floors and can be viewed at Lapicida's new London showroom. Prices start from £474sq m.

 TERRAZZO FLOOR TILES 3 of the best

1. Terrazzo Bosello Base, £156.30sq m, Fired Earth

2. Rialto Terrazzo in Santa Croce, £195sq m, Ca' Pietra at West One Bathrooms

3. Crisp Beige, £13.15 a tile, Topps Tiles

FEATURE HOLLY RANSOME

enduring appeal

Fancy recreating the rustic feel of a Mediterranean stone floor at home? Mandarin Stone has recently launched its Seville range including tiles that replicate the colour and appearance of terracotta. The matte tiles look and feel like baked earth, but are made from porcelain, a durable material that requires no specialist treatments, offering an accessible way to elevate your home with the timeless look of terracotta. The tiles are available in three shades of earthy brown as well as a milky white, plus a handful of traditional hand-painted patterns (pictured here is the Lola). Prices start from £40.77sq m. →

natural beauty

New to the offering of the Italian family-run company Florim is its Coretech collection celebrating the Piasentina stone found in the foothills of the Julian Alps in Friuli. Organically striking with its white-veined surface, the Calcarenite Piasentina stone has been used since Roman times. Florim processes the material to make its tiles more structurally sound, enhancing practicality and longevity. They are available in four shades of warm grey – pictured are the Flame Dark Matte (floor) tiles with the Satin Dark Soft tiles (kitchen island). Prices are available on request.

INSPIRED BY THE LAKES

Iris Ceramica took inspiration from the slate found in Cumbria for its latest flooring launch, namely Burlington stone, which has been produced in the area for over 450 years. Iris Ceramica's Victorian Stone porcelain recaptures the sandy textured quality that is found in the Lake District stone, yet it is easy to clean and boasts impressive resistance to wear. It's available in five colours. Prices start from £55sq m.

MARBLE MOOD

Italian company Ariostea has launched a beautiful emulation of Cremo Italia, the precious Italian marble found in the Apuan Alps. The porcelain stoneware replicates the delicate veined ivory look of the marble and is a practical and hard-wearing option. The tiles come in five different sizes. Prices start from £74.90sq m.

SOURCEBOOK

Other great places to find floor tiles

▪ BERT & MAY

The tile expert offers many beautiful patterned and plain stone tiles inspired by traditional Spanish design in sophisticated palettes, including reclaimed options.
bertandmay.com

▪ CLAYBROOK

Head here for contemporary and stylish floor tiles. Particularly lovely is the brand's recently launched Formella, made from recycled materials, with a matte appearance in a range of delectable colours.
claybrookstudio.co.uk

▪ GRANBY WORKSHOP

The Liverpool-based ceramic manufacturer at Granby specialises in recycled tiles with a distinctive colourful marbled appearance.
granbyworkshop.co.uk

▪ LASSCO

Master of reclamation, Lassco sources valuable materials from demolition sites – and it's the place to go for unique and environmentally friendly options such as Victorian terracotta, antique marble and salvaged encaustic tiles.
lassco.co.uk

▪ MARAZZI

Founded in 1935 in Sassuolo, Marazzi knows a thing or two about hard surfaces and has a broad range of stone, marble and concrete-effect tiles, including patterned and plains.
marazzitile.co.uk

▪ OTTO TILES & DESIGN

The founder of London-based Otto is inspired by the craftsmanship of her homeland, Turkey. We especially love the colourful mosaic zellige tiles.
ottotiles.co.uk 🄴

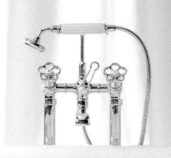

MADE BY HAND
TO LAST A LIFETIME

+44 (0)20 7376 4499
drummonds-uk.com

DRUMMONDS
LONDON · NEW YORK

Take a seat

Upholstered chairs for chic and comfortable dining

1.
2.
3.
4.
5.
6.
7.
8.
9.

1. Anbu in Natural, £325, Nkuku
2. Colton in Dark Brown leather, £2,850, Pinch
3. Belleville, £395 for a pair, Cox & Cox
4. Curvy, £1,415, Heaps & Woods
5. Nova in Green, £2,240, Fiona McDonald
6. Jennie, £595, Oka
7. Trellis in Fret Maze Blue Sky by Jim Thompson, from £960, Charles Orchard
8. Titus in Cane/Black oak, £640, Vincent Sheppard
9. Anais, £629, Heal's

FEATURE HOLLY RANSOME

Otto Sofa in Omega, Green Tea and Small Drum Stool in Paxton, Grey/Gold and Billy Footstool in Gus, Fen.

Made by one pair of hands in Britain | **arloandjacob.com** | 03300 945 855

Bath | Bristol | Ely | Guildford | Harrogate | Islington | Marlow | Melbourne | Solihull | St Albans | Tunbridge Wells | Wilmslow

Movers & Shakers

A deep-rooted love and respect for nature ensures the
work of Onno Adriaanse is full of expression

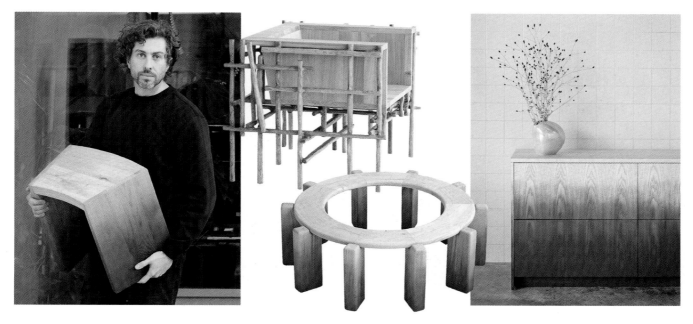

(Above, from left) Onno Adriaanse; the Hedera armchair is inspired by climbing plants, while the Dawn
collection, which features gradient colour, takes its cue from the tranquillity of early mornings

FOR Dutch furniture designer Onno Adriaanse, the starting point for every piece is nature. 'I've always been fascinated by geological processes, as well as flora and fauna,' he says. 'As a child, I had my own "museum" filled with rocks, dried plants and more, and that fascination remains. I love studying how trees grow, how stones are shaped by erosion, and the shape of an insect's shell. These forms, colours and textures inspire my designs.'

Having grown up in a creative family – his father owned an art gallery and his mother was a musician and ran a fashion boutique – he studied at the Design Academy Eindhoven in the Netherlands before setting up his own business in 2016. 'My parents took me and my sisters to museums all over the world, so from a young age I was drawing, painting and building things. The idea of imagining something in your head and then creating it with your hands captivated me then and still does today,' he says. 'In my teens, I was obsessed with the Bauhaus period and I collected second-hand, tubular frame furniture. Then during my studies, I learned I could create my own rules – why should a chair have four legs? Once I realised I could meld art with furniture design, everything clicked into place.'

Now based in an old industrial building in Eindhoven alongside 180 other creatives, he uses manual, machine and digital processes to create his designs, as well as bespoke finishes for interior architects or private clients. 'But craftsmanship always takes the lead,' he continues. 'I primarily work with solid wood – my favourite is elm, a typical Dutch tree with a wild and beautiful grain.'

Collaboration is also key, and current projects include the development of pieces alongside London-based marble studio Agglomerati, and Table du Sud, a Dutch furniture company. A dream job would be to create a large-scale installation with a major brand. 'A flagship store interior, for instance, would be an amazing opportunity to combine designs and finishes on a grand scale. With all my work, the goal is to create environments where people can slow down away from the speed of the digital age and instead focus on tranquillity.' &
onnoadriaanse.nl

"Every material has unique qualities,
but I love how each plank has its
own story shaped entirely by nature"

The Greco-Gothic Lopen Joinery Kitchen by Ben Pentreath Studio

You're cordially invited...

Head to Design Centre, Chelsea Harbour this summer to immerse yourself in WOW!house, on from 3 June to 3 July – we have a preview of three of the rooms created by renowned designers

LOPEN JOINERY KITCHEN BY BEN PENTREATH STUDIO

Stepping away from the 'watered-down' neo-Georgian cabinetry so prevalent in modern spaces, this colourful Greco-Gothic kitchen will celebrate the detailing and materials found 'below stairs' in English country houses. Ben Pentreath director Rupert Cunningham is working with Leo Kary and Alice Montgomery to create 'the least fitted kitchen possible'. The feel chimes with the studio's approach 'where each piece is connected through subtle design markers like they have been collected and curated rather designed by the same hand'.

NUCLEUS MEDIA ROOM BY ALEX DAULEY

Relaxing and opulent with a hint of drama is how Alex Dauley describes her approach to the design of this empty-nester, adults-only media room filled with gorgeous designs, objects and materials that those with young families probably wouldn't risk investing in but now, as the children have moved out, they can. 'I imagined myself as the client as I wanted it to feel authentic and not too lofty,' explains Alex. Design highlights include a generous sofa made by Julian Chichester and a rug by Holland & Sherry.

FORTUNY + BONACINA + BAROVIER&TOSO PRIMARY BEDROOM BY TOMÈF DESIGN

Tommaso Franchi has turned to his homeland and collaborated with three of Italy's prestige brands to create this bedroom inspired by 'the classic elegance of Venice'. The setting is a suite with a living and sleeping area, where traditions and heritage have been reinterpreted with a modern eye. Look out for the Tiara bed combining the artistry of all three brands with a rattan frame ('pointing to the history of trade with the East'), gold velvet and a drop-shaped Murano glass jewel at the pinnacle. See dcch.co.uk

FEATURE ARABELLA YOUENS **ILLUSTRATIONS** (KITCHEN) LUKAS PALUMBO @LUKASTHEILLUSTRATOR; (MEDIA ROOM) TANATSWA BORERWE, (BEDROOM) TOMÈF DESIGN

The sophisticated
Nucleus Media Room
by Alex Dauley

A sumptuous space
with an Italian
design stamp:
Fortuny + Bonacina
+ Barovier&Toso
Primary Bedroom
by Tomèf Design

Design & Decorating
MAKING BEAUTIFUL SPACES FOR JOYFUL LIVING

COLOUR OF THE MONTH
'This orange limewash paint by Bauwerk is called Grevillea, named after an Australian flower. The room's earthy palette is rooted in nature, conjuring a feeling of serenity. There's an eclecticism to the layering of the pieces, with the rich terracotta walls offset by the icy Arctic desk from Sister by Studio Ashby,' says Sophie Ashby, founder and creative director, Studio Ashby. Walls in Grevillea, £36 for 1ltr, Bauwerk →

A look at the shade of orange gracing the most exquisite interiors, how travel is having a beautiful influence on decoration, a directory of European brands producing iconic furniture and more

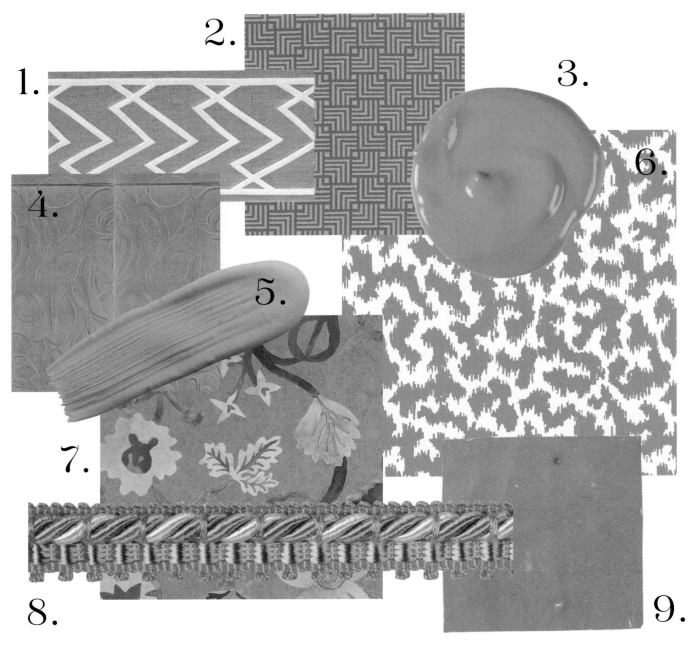

PHOTOGRAPHS (JOYFUL CANVAS) JONATHAN BOND. (SUNSET GLOW) CHRIS HORWOOD. (GROUNDING WARMTH) LINDSAY BROWN

COLOUR OF THE MONTH

FIERY ORANGE

1. Summit appliqué tape in Coral, £54m, Thibaut
2. Sophie fabric in Ruggine, £153m, Teorema collection at Rubelli
3. Coral Orange No. 277 marble matt emulsion, £64.50 for 2.5ltr, Mylands
4. Colosse Fruitier wallcovering in RM 1090 31, £958 per panel (H3.2mxW1.18m), Le Jardin d'Aloès collection at Élitis
5. Carly's Loafers matt emulsion, £45 for 2.5ltr, Claybrook
6. Fez wallpaper in Spice, £120 a roll, Warner House
7. Catalpha wallpaper in Sanquina, £164 a roll, Casa Natuendo at The Fabric Collective
8. Marquises gimp in Terre de Feu, 14mm, £16.80m, Houlès
9. Orange Zellige tile, £142.80sq m, Otto Tiles & Design

JOYFUL CANVAS

'For this snug TV room we wanted a warm yet cheerful colour. Malahide by Edward Bulmer Natural Paint is a versatile shade which works in dark or sunny rooms. It also makes a great backdrop for artwork – we've used it several times drenched over walls and joinery.'
Alex Keith, co-founder,
Otta Design

SUNSET GLOW

'I wanted this penthouse at Chelsea Barracks to have a sense of glamour so I selected Dedar's moiré Amoir Libre fabric wallcovering in Mandarine for its beautiful reflective qualities. It's a flattering shade, especially in candlelight, and it pairs well with greens and blues.'
Susie Atkinson, founder,
Studio Atkinson

GROUNDING WARMTH

'This beautiful Cotto tile from Clay Imports strikes the perfect balance between earthy and sophisticated. The orange feels instantly inviting, yet it holds its own as a design element – there's a timeless quality to it that we love. It also works well in kitchens and entryways.'
Annie Downing, founder,
Annie Downing Interiors 🔄

43

DECORATING

Sunshine state

Summer is on the horizon and the new-season
outdoor fabric collections offer brilliant
design possibilities for the garden

FEATURE PIPPA BLENKINSOP

Sitting pretty

(Opposite) Whether you have a large garden or a tiny terrace, patterned weatherproof fabrics are a wonderful way to elevate outdoor seating. Available in seven shades, Saona is a playful woven geometric featuring organic stripes and a slubby texture, which beautifully complements natural materials. **Armchairs in** Saona outdoor fabric in Ébène, £126m; **cushions in** Saona outdoor fabric in Anis, £126m, both Manuel Canovas

Lazy days

(Top) Bring a touch of the Côte d'Azur to the English garden with a tent in vibrant beach umbrella stripes, perfect for lazy afternoons shading from the midday sun or a joyful hideaway on a grey day. Available in an array of bold colours, Pierre Frey's new lightfast and stain-resistant Belvedere fabric will make a lasting impression. **Canopy and cushion in** Belvedere high-performance indoor/outdoor fabric in Soleil, £149m, Pierre Frey

Holiday cheer

(Bottom right) Fade-resistant saturated plains and bold graphic prints are ideal for warm climates where they remain eye-catching even in full sun. Paying homage to Portuguese culture, the Faro collection from Élitis combines plant-inspired jacquards with Moorish geometrics and practical plains bound in tones of garden green, sky blue and zesty yellow. **Lounger, cushion and curtain in** Nossa outdoor fabric OD 154 20, £192m; **green cushion in** Pedra outdoor fabric OD 156 63, £110m, both the Faro collection at Élitis

(Centre left) Borneo outdoor fabric 11085.36, £200m, Nobilis; (centre right) Ocala Stripe indoor/outdoor woven fabric in Clementine/Chalk, £58m, Harlequin; (bottom left) Colma indoor/outdoor fabric in Marigold, £210m, Schumacher →

Artisan appeal

(Top left) Renowned for its hand-block-printed linens, Walter G has translated a number of its designs into woven Sunbrella acrylic fabrics perfect for capturing the artisan aesthetic in exterior spaces. Inspired by rustic textiles, Dash Dot and Balos make playful alternatives to timeless stripes.
Bench cushions in Dash Dot Sunbrella acrylic fabric in Rattan, £197.40m; **inner cushions in** Balos Sunbrella acrylic fabric in Papaya, £197.40m, both Walter G at The Fabric Collective

Sun-baked warmth

(Centre right) New from Casamance, the Hozho outdoor collection pays homage to the textile traditions of the Navajo with a spirited mix of chevron weaves, textural plains and tactile abstract patterns. Available in warm neutrals to rich blues and terracottas, the fabrics look wonderful against surfaces in earthy, sun-baked tones.
Bench seat in Serapes outdoor fabric in Turquoise, £104.30m, the Hozho collection at Casamance; Hozho **outdoor cushions** in Terracotta, £71.30 each, Maison Casamance

Layered lounging

(Bottom) For laid-back seating with a relaxed holiday feel try low-level benches topped with plenty of cushions in warm, earthy fabrics. With a focus on comfort and softness, the Al Fresco II collection from George Spencer Designs features three complementary geometric weaves, which can be combined to create welcoming outdoor living spaces with a depth to rival indoor schemes.
Bench cushions in Hopscotch 5 outdoor fabric, £172m; **large scatter cushions in** Puzzle 1 and 5 outdoor fabric, £140m; **small cushions in** Zig Zag 5 outdoor fabric, £172m, all solution-dyed polypropylene from the Al Fresco II collection at George Spencer Designs

Make a splash

(Opposite) Whether used over simple garden seating or statement poolside cabana curtains, eye-catching multitone beach stripes are a timeless and joyful choice for exterior use. With jewel-toned bands of cornflower blue, hot pink and lush green, the new Esprit Stripe fabric from Thibaut would sit beautifully in the summer garden paired with tropical prints.
Cabana/canopy in Esprit Stripe indoor/outdoor fabric in Cornflower and Peony, £162m; **cushion in** Protea Print indoor/outdoor fabric in Navy, £153m, both Thibaut

(Top right) Sicily recycled polyester indoor/outdoor fabric in Green, £170m, Fermoie; (centre left) Samarkand outdoor fabric in Spice, £55m, Warner House →

Taste of the Med

(Opposite) Inspired by the cascading foliage hanging from Capri's colonnades, Capri Flora is a woven jacquard featuring stylised leaves designed by Italian architect and interior designer Giuliano Andrea dell'Uva. Available in vibrant ocean blues or botanical greens, pair the lively leafy linen with pops of zesty lemon and cane seating for a magical alfresco dining setting.
Tablecloth in Capri Flora outdoor fabric 10790.111, £356.40m, Giuliano Andrea dell'Uva for Fischbacher 1819

Classic florals

(Top) Decorative fabrics needn't be reserved for indoors, with a wide array of performance patterns available you can create layered outdoor living spaces with equal wow factor. Combining heritage design with weatherproof materials, the new Indoor Outdoor Weaves collection from Morris & Co. features eight classic Morris & Co. patterns reimagined as woven performance fabrics in fresh, fade-resistant colour palettes.
Sofa in Wardle Weave in Mineral Blue, £140m with **cushion in** Acorn Weave in Mineral Blue, £122m; **left armchair in** Acorn Weave in Mineral Blue, £122m with **cushion in** Bird & Anemone Weave in Teal, £122m; **right armchair in** Bird & Anemone Weave in Teal, £122m, with **cushion in** Wardle Weave in Mineral Blue, £140m; **stools in** Thistle Weave in River Wandle, £122m, all Morris & Co.

Into the blue

(Centre right) Naturally at home amid lush greenery, fabrics with bold beautiful blooms will bring sunshine whatever the weather. Comprising modern meandering tropical designs to iconic ditsy florals and small-scale geometrics, The Liberty Garden Collection translates the eclectic spirit of the heritage brand into durable performance fabric.
Loungers in Fantasia Jungle Easton outdoor fabric in Lapis, £120m; **parasol in** Betsy Flora Easton outdoor fabric in Lapis, £120m, both The Liberty Garden Collection by Liberty

Plain sailing

(Bottom left) Subtle, textural plains are guaranteed to complement any outdoor area. Perfect for bringing luxurious comfort and colour to chic alfresco seating, the Vacation & Riviera collection from Zinc Textile features soft bouclé weaves specially designed to be UV-, water- and stain-resistant. Choose from versatile neutrals to soothing ocean teals.
Left stool in Grimaud Outdoor bouclé in Teal, £90m; **right stool in** Corniche Outdoor bouclé in Teal, £96m, both Zinc Textile

(Centre left) Ozone outdoor printed fabric in Prato, £115m, Christopher Farr Cloth; (bottom right) Cornucopia outdoor fabric in Ionian Sea, £142m, Madeaux by Richard Smith 🖰

EUROPEAN FURNITURE

So many iconic pieces hail from Europe
– these are just a few of the brands that
continue to produce standout designs

Pacha lounge
chair, from
£2,299; Wonder
sofa, from
£4,999; Semi
pendant lights,
£449 each,
all Gubi

A &TRADITION

Built upon Denmark's revered design legacy, Copenhagen's &Tradition came onto the furniture scene in 2010. Honouring historic pieces as well as the modern-day avant-garde, its product library spans the 1930s to the contemporary, its roster of designers ranging from the great Arne Jacobsen to current names such as Anderssen & Voll, Jaime Hayon, Luca Nichetto, Mia Hamborg and Note Design Studio.
andtradition.com

ATELIER VIME

Named after a word derived from the Latin 'vimen', meaning a flexible branch for weaving, Atelier Vime is the go-to place for rattan and wicker design. Hailing from French village Vallabrègues, the brand was founded in 1878 when it began to build a collection of 20th-century pieces. It soon connected with artisans, now providing in-house created furniture and smaller items.
ateliervime.com

AUDO

Denmark's Audo (established in 1978 under previous name, Menu) emphasises the importance of human connection and a sense of community, which is brought together in its Copenhagen HQ, Audo House. The building hosts a concept store, restaurant and hotel, created as a hub for ideas and inspiration as well as to showcase furniture designs.
audocph.com

B BONTEMPI

Balancing Italy's lauded craft heritage with innovation to create timelessly chic furniture, Bontempi

Standard collection, Francesco Binfaré for Edra

was initially a metal workshop when founded in 1963, before pivoting into the table, seating, storage, desk, console and lighting manufacturer we know today. Based in the town of Camerano, the firm epitomises the spirit of 'Made in Italy' design with its comfortable, functional take on beauty and artisanal excellence. Shown below is the Bach table by Andrea Lucatello, price on request.
bontempi.it

D DE LA ESPADA

Found nestled in forest near Portugal's Silver Coast, De La Espada creates seating, beds and storage in its solar-powered factory. An expert in solid wood, the brand combines the handmaking skills of artisans with advanced machinery. Founded in 1993, its aesthetic stems from influences including the Arts and Crafts movement, 1950s Scandinavian design and architects such as Tadao Ando, Luis Barragán, John Pawson. Collaborating with designers including Neri&Hu, StudioIlse, Matthew Hilton

and Luca Nichetto, the company's collection is unified by a sense of warmth, pared-back beauty and deep respect for timber.
delaespada.com

E EDRA

Focused on comfort, elegance and quality, furniture maker Edra was born in 1987 in Italy's Tuscany. Amalgamating artistic flair, manual expertise and craft knowledge with technological research, the brand's bold chairs, tables, sofas, beds and cabinets are mould-breaking and head-turning, existing as both functional and sculptural objects. Its Flap and On the Rocks sofas can adapt to the needs of different people and spaces by changing shape.
edra.com

EIKUND

Turning attention back to a golden era of Norwegian furniture is 2016-founded Eikund, which hunts out, revives and relaunches iconic lounge chairs by mid-century designers from the country, such as Sigurd Resell, Arne Tjomsland and Sven Ivar Dysthe. Based in southern village Hellvik, the brand delves into archives to uncover rare and forgotten chair treasures from the 1950s and 1960s, respectfully bringing them back to life via exquisite artisanry and natural materials.
eikund.com →

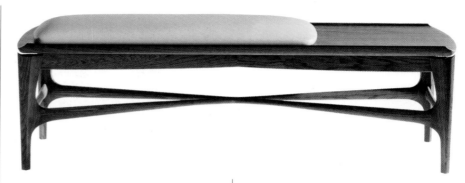

F FOGIA

Swedish company Fogia selects the timber it uses for its stools, chairs, tables and storage while the trees are still growing in forests close to its factory to minimise transportation, after which each piece is crafted by experts. From its Stockholm HQ, the 1981-founded brand collaborates with contemporary designers such as Inga Sempé, Note Design Studio and Norm Architects as well as designing in-house, rooting its aesthetic in classic Nordic style alongside modern charm and an avant-garde touch.
fogia.com

G GUBI

Positioning itself at the point where 'the beauty of history meets the thrill of right now', 1967-founded Copenhagen firm Gubi's furniture is about both curating the classics and working with designers to develop icons of the future. 'Creativity and playfulness are at the heart of everything we do,' says chief brand officer Marie Kristine Schmidt. From legends such as Gio Ponti, Greta M. Grossman, Gabriella Crespi and Joe Colombo to contemporary names

including Space Copenhagen, OEO Studio and GamFratesi, its sculptural pieces are a celebration of the best of 20th-century design and onwards.
gubi.com

L LAURA GONZALEZ

French architect and interior designer Laura Gonzalez opened a furniture gallery in Paris in 2022, creating pieces originally seen in her Normandy home. She now works on seating, tables and smaller items that reflect the aesthetic of the spaces she designs, known for their dynamic combinations of motifs, materials and colours, combined with an aura of classic romanticism and a captivating narrative.
lauragonzalez.fr

Laura Gonzalez is known for her use of rich patterns and playful details

LIGNE ROSET

The firm is noted for experimenting with materials as well as creating furniture that's both visually striking and comfortable. Founded in 1860 in French village Montagnieu, Ligne Roset initially produced wooden umbrellas, walking sticks and chairs for local markets before transforming into the bold maker we know today. Its furniture designs are defined by a mixture of chicness and innovation.
ligne-roset.com

M MODET

Representing for the Republic of Ireland is Cork-based Modet. The family business has a refined collection of chairs, tables and a bed, all designed with flowing lines and curves and created with both western and Japanese shaping tools. Each piece is made to order by a team of skilled craftspeople from solid wood and can be customised in alternate timbers, sizes and upholstery options. Shown above is the Langford bench, £3,750.
modet.ie

MOOOI

Dutch brand Moooi – the bonus 'o' is to signify 'something extra' – defines itself as rebellious, eclectic, unexpected and original. Founded by designer Marcel Wanders and Casper Vissers in 2001 and based in Breda in the Netherlands, the brand creates bold, whimsical designs that feel theatrical as well as elegant. Its seating, tables and storage are akin to characterful pieces of art, the imaginative forms created with innovative construction techniques.
moooi.com

MUUTO

Copenhagen's Muuto is centred around the mantra of 'new perspectives' (which is what its name means in Finnish). The 2006-established Danish brand builds on classic Scandinavian design heritage while at the same time looking towards the future. Its skilfully crafted seating, tables, storage and more are united by a style that stands out while evoking an age-proof feel.
muuto.com

Stacked Oak storage system, £573, Julien De Smedt for Muuto

N NEW WORKS

Paying homage to Scandinavian furniture-making is New Works, the Copenhagen brand dedicated to bold, shapely forms, while respecting the natural qualities of the materials it uses for its seating, sofas, beds and storage. Debuting in 2015, it aims to challenge current design zeitgeist to bring fresh forms and materials into the home, working alongside designers such as Anderssen & Voll, Lim + Lu, Steven Bukowski, Panter & Tourron, Cristián Mohaded, Hunting & Narud.
newworks.dk

O ORIGIN MADE

'Each piece bears an invisible thread that connects its designer to its maker and to its user,' says Porto-based craft-focused furniture producer Origin Made, which was inspired by local artisanal traditions

PHOTOGRAPHS (NEW WORKS) BRIAN BUCHARD, 2024

and founded in 2017. Working with family-run workshops and artificers across Portugal and Spain, the brand creates small-batch stools, plinths, benches, chairs, tables and cabinets, aiming to nurture a greater appreciation for tactility, materiality and the handmaking process. Shown above is the Évora side table, £1,447.
origin-made.com

P PAPADATOS

Flying the flag for Greece is Athens' Papadatos, which came to the fore in 1990 specialising in crafting sofas, armchairs and modular seating, as well as tables and storage. Pieces are shapely, minimal and modern, designed to coordinate with each other and coexist in harmony. Seating is both contemporary and contoured while also emphasising ergonomics and the immersive experience of comfort.
papadatos.gr

PARLA

With a rich and impressive history, Turkey's Parla started out producing furniture for the Ottoman Empire in 1910 (including for a Royal Palace). The Istanbul-based brand has always combined the latest technologies with a respect for time-honoured techniques and expertise. The company's seating, tables and storage are modern and striking while having a sense of

delicate artistry about them, the pieces created by highly experienced traditional artisans working with high-tech machinery in a balance of design, craft skill and manufacture.
parladesign.com

PETITE FRITURE

Parisian brand Petite Friture is imbued with jovial joy de vivre, curating an interiors universe filled with the unusual, the daring and occasionally the surreal. Its diverse collection includes chairs, tables, sofas, lighting and accessories and features pieces by over 60 renowned and up-and-coming designers including Studiopepe, Daniel Emma, Carole Baijings, Constance Guisset, Färg & Blanche and Noé Duchaufour-Lawrance.
petitefriture.com

POLIFORM

Founded in northern Italy's iconic Brianza furniture district in 1970 – the evolution of a small artisan business from the 1940s – Poliform crafts contemporary bookcases, storage solutions, wardrobes, sofas and beds, as well as kitchens and indoor architectural systems. The designs are united by their sleek, pared-back aesthetic which exudes both luxury and serenity, the brand partnering with an impressive ensemble of celebrated designers.
poliform.it →

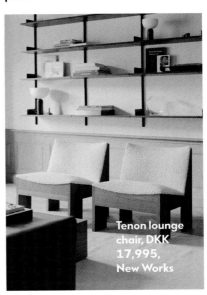

Tenon lounge chair, DKK 17,995, New Works

PORADA

For Porada, it all comes down to a love of wood. The Como-based Italian brand began producing chairs in 1948 and is now renowned for its impeccably crafted wood, typically its signature Canaletta walnut, which it shapes into forms that seem to defy gravity. Its chairs, tables and beds are both elegant and evocative, often pushing timber to its limits to create shapes that loop, twist and flow. **porada.it**

R RIMADESIO

Residing in Italian furniture-making hotspot Brianza, Rimadesio designs standalone pieces plus modular systems, sliding panels, walk-in wardrobes and more. Exploring technological innovations and prioritising research, the 1956-founded brand is expert at partitioning space in an intelligent and modern way. Below is the Rialto coffee table, €1,103 plus VAT. **rimadesio.it**

ROCHE BOBOIS

Since its inception in 1960, Paris-based Roche Bobois has zeroed in on creative furniture. Following French art de vivre – the philosophy of enjoying life's pleasures with elegance – its refined range of seating, tables, beds and storage is full of colour and surprise. **roche-bobois.com**

Titus dining armchairs, £665 each; Ari dining table, £3,375; Arvin pendant lamps, from £415 each, all Vincent Sheppard

T THE SOCIALITE FAMILY

Initially a lifestyle platform curating homes, fashion and design before transforming into an interiors brand in 2017, France's The Socialite Family makes furniture in response to how the modern family lives; with their homes as stages for memories and creativity. Designed in Paris and crafted by meticulous artisans across Europe, its pieces aim to 'restore the sublime to the everyday'. **thesocialitefamily.com**

TON

Operating since 1861, Ton's HQ in Czech Republic town Bystřice pod Hostýnem still uses the traditional technique of steam-bending wood. The brand is known for its 1850s-designed Number 14 chair by Michael Thonet – regarded as the world's first mass-produced piece of furniture – and a host of other recognisable works that have become embedded into society. **ton.eu**

V VINCENT SHEPPARD

Founded in 1992 to honour and preserve the tradition of Lloyd Loom weaving, Vincent Sheppard has become a global leader in furniture crafted with the technique (where twisted kraft paper is wrapped around a metal wire and shaped). Based in Belgian city Kortrijk, the brand's chairs and tables are contemporary and understated as well as being lightweight and durable. **vincentsheppard.com**

W WITTMANN

Austrian company Wittmann is focused on new ideas and forms rather than an overall aesthetic for its sofas, chairs and tables, which it's been producing since the 1950s (the brand formed in 1896 as a saddlery). Furniture is made with expertise by local artisans, materials sourced from its locale and the ideas of designers such as Jaime Hayon, Sebastian Herkner and Luca Nichetto. **wittmann.at**

ART & SOUL

Our columnist Willow Kemp on how paintings and other creative forms are the heart of a space

As design director for Kit Kemp Design Studio and art ambassador for Firmdale Hotels, and having studied architecture at Cambridge and sculpture in Germany, Willow is well-versed in anything art-related.

❝ Art is often the first thing someone notices when they enter a room. It captures their attention and imagination and leaves an impression. Art is the keystone of creativity in interior design. It is centre to my design ethos and approach, with every project being shaped by its own carefully curated pieces.

Allowing art to guide you in the design process isn't just practical, it gives a space meaning. Interesting interiors always combine functional design with expressive and emotive art. The two disciplines are inextricably linked, influencing each other – and when successfully executed, they enhance each other.

Art can impact space without even being present. You don't have to own a piece to create a scheme led by art; furniture forms inspired by an Antony Gormley sculpture or a colour scheme dictated by a Paul Klee painting are evocative starting points for an interior.

A work of art will immediately set the mood of an interior, giving it character and a narrative. It adds colour, texture and form and provides a starting point from which you can select your colour palette, fabrics and furniture. You can use art as a framework for the space, as a guide to position furniture. It can also act as a focal point, to accentuate a beautiful fireplace or disguise less desirable architectural features.

Art can tie the elements in a space together making it coherent, but you can also incorporate it outside the frame by having fun translating patterns and shapes from artwork into textiles and rugs. Perhaps appliqué a shape or feature from an artwork on the back of a chair or cushion, picking out thread colours to match or complement the art. You can embellish furniture using stencils as a guide in the same way that furniture designer Tom Faulkner began – he now creates coveted sculptural pieces. Hand-painted murals enveloping a whole interior are artworks in themselves, but you can achieve a similar effect with wallpaper murals, such as Kit Kemp's Mythical Land design.

The work of artists inspires textiles, furniture and lighting designs as well. Take a look at Vanderhurd's hand-dyed rugs, Christopher Farr Cloth's textiles capturing the creative essence of renowned artists such as Sandra Blow or Anni Albers, and Margit Wittig's bronze and resin lighting, which has a nod to Brâncuşi and Giacometti. I recently visited designer Laura Gonzalez's showroom in New York, where a relief fireplace by ceramist Laurent Dufour and the Himawari floor lamp resembling a playful oversized flower bring an artistic feel without being a formal or traditional presentation of art.

The art someone chooses to live with reflects their character and it inadvertently has the power to shape them too. You will often find that successful interior designers have a passion for collecting art because within objects, paintings and sculpture you can find inspiration. They don't have to be masterpieces – in fact, they can be very ordinary – but art helps to create a rhythm to a space and to animate it. It is clear that the greats of interior design listen to their instincts when they are designing and curating art. They are open-minded and unafraid to make mistakes – and that helps with their creativity.

Buildings and their interiors are essentially evolutionary, so don't worry about trying to create a finite entity in your home. Accept that spaces evolve over time. Art can be dynamic and versatile – arranging and rearranging pieces can completely change how a space feels. I often find that over the journey a project takes, order becomes chaos and then returns to order again. Realise the importance of imperfection: juxtapose old objects next to new ones, expensive ones next to inexpensive ones, and you'll discover that the relationship between them will add interest.

When you align art with interior design, a space becomes more than the sum of its parts – I like to think of it as bringing friends together at a party. Art animates a room, changing our experience of it and enabling us to communicate what words cannot. It is the cohesive thread, tying a space together. Art is not the final flourish or an afterthought – it is the soul of the place. ❞ 🅖

PHOTOGRAPHS (PORTRAIT OF WILLOW, KIT KEMP DESIGN STUDIO) SIMON BROWN. (AXEL VERVOORDT) LAZIZ HAMANI WITH ARTWORK BY MICHAËL BORREMANS

Willow says it is clear that interior design greats listen to their instincts when it comes to art

Octavia Dickinson's layered approach to incorporating art feels curated and creative

Kit Kemp is an expert in artistic interiors and uses artworks of every kind in her projects

Axel Vervoordt commissioned a life-sized painting of his horse by artist Michaël Borremans

THREE DESIGNERS WHO UNDERSTAND THE POWER OF ART

OCTAVIA DICKINSON

Octavia draws on her background in art history and a deep understanding of how important context is for each individual piece of work and what it can bring to an interior. She approaches a room like a beautiful painting, combining shapes and colours in compositions that delight the senses.

AXEL VERVOORDT

He has a rich take on simplicity. It's not minimalist, but everything Axel hangs or places in an interior is there for a purpose. I'd love to visit his restored 12th-century castle in the Belgium countryside, where each room has a different mood and he can travel through time in his own property.

KIT KEMP

There are seminal pieces in Kit's art collection, but is also has some that are there to add character and make you look twice. She has a natural instinct for discovering emerging artists and curating colourful and joyful interiors that celebrate art in all forms.

Wallpaper · Fabric · Sampling · Soft Furnishings · Bespoke Curtains & Blinds

wallpaperdirect.com

TREND - 'Striped Blooms' featuring :

Mavis - Wear the Walls | Tulip Wave - Sophie Harpley | Pipkin Stripe - Albany | Foxglove Stripe - Graham & Brown

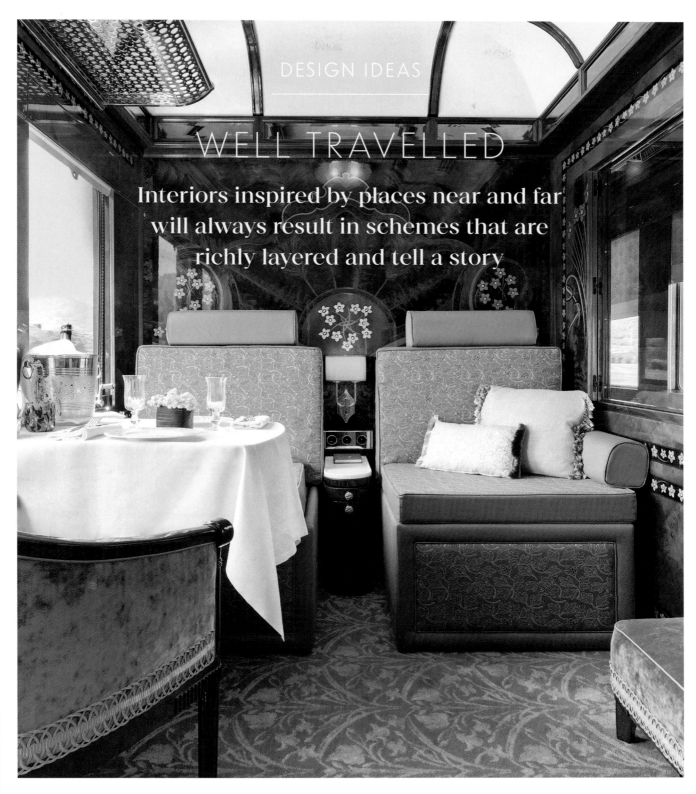

DESIGN IDEAS

WELL TRAVELLED

Interiors inspired by places near and far
will always result in schemes that are
richly layered and tell a story

FEATURE ARABELLA YOUENS PHOTOGRAPH LUDOVIC BALAY

FIRST CLASS

In the 1920s, the Orient Express began its journey to Istanbul ushering in what is now regarded as the heyday of luxury rail journeys – and the inspiration behind one or two murder-mystery novels. When the owner, Belmond, decided to upgrade the historic carriages into suites with bathrooms, they asked fabric house Rubelli to help. The team, working with Wimberly Interiors, created bespoke jacquards in rich colours to dress the suites on the Venice Simplon-Orient-Express. Other decorative details include art deco lights by Lalique and wood panelling adorned with marquetry. At night chairs convert into beds. →

EASTERN PROMISE

Juxtaposing different design styles or introducing something unexpected will always result in an interesting, layered space. This bedroom, designed by interior decorator and textile designer Penny Morrison, was for a house in Barbados. And yet, she's used a four-poster bed with a distinctively Chinese accent both in its form and also the lacquered red paint. Alongside this, she's used a botanical fabric on the curtains and one of her own table lamps. 'Dreaming of lying in bed in a world of patterns and colours, this bedroom from a project we did in Barbados in 2021 depicts how prints and patterns can be juxtaposed to create harmonious spaces,' says Penny.

PHOTOGRAPH MIKE GARLICK

SWEDISH CROWN

While houses that pre-date central heating will more often than not feature fireplaces as focal points in rooms, a wood-burning stove will have a similar visual impact. Circular tiled stoves are traditional Swedish designs, known as kakelugn, which often feature ornate or elaborate embellishments such as crowns at the top. This scheme was designed by Olivia Outred. With the white, minimally decorated walls, seagrass rug, rattan chairs and acid yellow cushions and the stove with its brass doors, she's introduced a confident touch of Abba-era glamour into the room. 'We wanted to create a light but warm space,' says Olivia. 'The stove is a Karl-Johan model [typical of the turn-of-the-century designs], imported from Sweden,' she adds.

TIME TRAVEL

Japonisme was a 19th-century craze for Japanese art and design in western Europe. For more than 40 years, it inspired designers in the furthest reaches of the world and then morphed into two aesthetic movements: art nouveau and art deco. This hand-painted wallpaper by de Gournay is an ode to the art deco movement – cranes were a motif seen frequently throughout the era. Used here, it envelops a corner of the firm's premises in Los Angeles, at once introducing a decadent and glamorous atmosphere. Evoking the artwork of Jean Dunand, the wallpaper is illustrated in a three-dimensional gold leaf that is then tarnished and burnished to create the impression of light breaking through the clouds. →

PHOTOGRAPHS (TIME TRAVEL) MICHAEL CLIFFORD

"Unique trinkets and objets d'art from far-flung destinations make up some of our most valuable possessions"

MARTIN WALLER, founder of Andrew Martin

MIAMI INFLUENCES

Vibrant colours, organic textures and curved shapes are essential ingredients for designing a cool and arty living space. Here, mid-century rattan chairs, colourful canvases and a collection of ceramics bring character to the living room of a 1920s house in Coral Gables, Miami, decorated by Natalia Miyar. This room has three windows – which look out to a leafy view – and Natalia's use of colour and shapes helps to bring the garden inside. 'This living room has all the hallmarks of my work,' says Natalia. 'It celebrates the architecture, the vibrant landscape and the individuality that comes from designing with statement pieces of vintage, contemporary furniture and well-chosen works of art.'

SELECTED SOUVENIRS

The Victorians, with their cabinets of curiosity and penchant for spending new-found wealth on travels, were keen to show off treasures and did so typically using vitrines. Hiding something behind glass has a touch of museum-like coldness to it so an alternative is using a table or shelves to display a collection. Joint managing director of Sibyl Colefax & John Fowler Philip Hooper has created a tableau of pieces in his home, including bowls, ceramics and metalwork. Here, antique Moroccan tooled leather panels sit either side of a Queen Anne–style mirror from Jeremy Rothman. The table was designed by Philip for John Stefanidis, and the ceramics are from his travels. Together, the pieces are set off by the walls in Little Greene's Canton.

PHOTOGRAPHS (MIAMI INFLUENCES) NICOLE FRANZEN. (SELECTED SOUVENIRS) SIMON BROWN

TOUCH OF TROPICS

That nature should be brought inside as much as possible is a mantra for many who recommend using multiple shades of green alongside botanical prints to achieve the desired look. Using tropical references takes things one step further. Rooms by interior designer Nina Litchfield typically display hints of her Brazilian roots and German upbringing alongside design cues inherited from her mother who loved traditional English interiors – and that's very much the case in her west London home. In the drawing room, a green leopard–print sofa and colourful painting root this space invitingly in another world. →

BEAUTIFULLY TONED

The results of colour drenching are immersive and bravely commit the space in one design direction. In this cigar room for a London home, design studio Banda chose Bauwerk Colour's Hazelnut to drench the walls and ceiling. Combined with Dedar's distinctive Tiger Mountain curtain fabric, Andy Warhol's *Siberian Tiger* print and the zebra-print bowl, the result is moody and atmospheric. 'Inspired by travels to the Far East, Banda designed this cosy, authentic feeling cigar room, which has a masculine, moody, rich atmosphere as might be found in the most luxurious tiger lodge retreat,' says founder Edo Mapelli Mozzi.

FRENCH FARMHOUSE

Collections of blue and white china have long been a favourite choice for kitchen displays and they look especially attractive when paired with antique delft tiles, as shown in this scheme. '[This is] one of our favourite projects to date – a pretty arts and crafts riverside cottage in London,' says interior designer Susie Atkinson, founder of Studio Atkinson. While the kitchen is completely new, it was made to look as if it had always been there. 'The antique sink, found in France, was restored and installed, and antique delft tiles were shipped over to make the perfect backdrop for the client's gorgeous plate collection.' The island unit was made bespoke by Rupert Bevan.

STORY TELLING

While perfectly curated interiors are tempting, many believe that rooms should show evidence of real life. 'Homes don't tell stories any more,' laments designer Christopher Howe. For this scheme in Berkshire, he addressed this issue. Called the 'Penguin Room', owing to the client's vast collection of Penguin paperbacks, he has furnished the office-come-withdrawing room (the desk is out of sight) with components that speak of the owner's life and experiences, including a penguin from the Falklands and an impressive image of huddled penguins in Antarctica. 'The only out-of-bounds area to the children, this withdrawing room stands at the back of the house and is part of the original building, dating back to the 1600s,' he says. →

PHOTOGRAPHS (FRENCH FARMHOUSE) SIMON BROWN. (STORY TELLING) CLAUDIA ROCHA

"The room is wrapped in Gucci Heron wallpaper and the concealed jib door means it's like a little secret surprise"

TIFFANY DUGGAN, founder of Studio Duggan

FOUND OBJECTS

While photographs, paintings and small objects are arguably easier to hang and display on a shelf, three-dimensional sculptural pieces, whether defined as high art or something more rustic, often have a transformative impact on a space; in short, they are too large to ignore. In the library of her 1930s house in Hampshire, creative director of Firmdale Hotels Kit Kemp has employed vivid colours and eye-catching patterns. Alongside, she displays timber pieces from very different backgrounds. Vast shields from Papua New Guinea stand alongside contemporary wooden sculptures and both sit comfortably alongside exposed oak beams. 'Despite the stylistic differences, they work well together as a collection because they are all in the same material,' says Kit.

BIG REVEAL

When it comes to decorating cloakrooms, many designers are tempted to take the more is more approach. A striking wallpaper celebrates individuality and, as they are both small spaces and ones that few spend much time in, it's often possible to push the boat out. This dramatic space, decorated in flamboyant Gucci Heron wallpaper, was designed by Tiffany Duggan, founder of Studio Duggan, for a house in Hertfordshire. Tiffany says that all restraint went out the window to create a magical, fun and whimsical home for a young family. 'The basin is pink onyx and the custom mirror was designed by us,' she says.

PHOTOGRAPH KENSINGTON LEVERNE

IMPERIAL ELEGANCE

Blending elements from different international styles and eras will often result in rooms that feel both intriguing and modern. In this guest bedroom by Studio Ashby for an apartment in Belgravia, scenes of Imperial China play out on the hand-painted wallpaper. The classical portrait in oil, complete with a gilded frame, sets a pleasing cultural contrast. 'While I love projects where I have creative freedom, this one challenged me to listen and adapt to my stylish French client's vision, blending her passion for historic French design with my expertise,' explains founder and creative director Sophie Ashby. →

CULTURE CLUB

When struggling to pick a colour scheme for a room, one place to look for inspiration is at any pictures and paintings that are likely to hang in the space. This family room in a Notting Hill house, designed by Studio Vero, features custom-upholstered stools and an ottoman, as well as a Model 54 armchair from Dagmar. The crawling ants sculptures are by Colombian artist Rafael Gomez Barros and the collage is by Georgie Hopton. 'Our scheme for this family room was informed by our client's art collection and their South American heritage,' explain the studio's co-founders Venetia Rudebeck and Romanos Brihi.

TRAVEL-INSPIRED INTERIORS

SOMETHING UNEXPECTED The joy of using inspiration from travels in decorating schemes is that it will almost always introduce something unique into a room. 'Travel is a constant source of inspiration for us in the Sims Hilditch studio,' says studio lead Gemma Holsgrove. 'We add to a scrapbook of ideas and use the results as a way of introducing something distinctive or unexpected to our projects.' There is also something charming about being surrounded by things that spark happy memories, says Sarah Peake, founder of Studio Peake. She's recently designed a chandelier, using beads hand-painted in Belgium, which began as an idea while on holiday in Greece. 'When I think about the things I've bought on my travels – some favourites being a painting in Suffolk, a candlestick in Stockholm, a jug from South Africa – they all spark a memory and transport me back to that place and moment in time.'

BLENDING DIFFERENT STYLES The eclectic nature of travel-inspired interiors is what makes them interesting, but keeping a consistent colour palette and vibrancy is important to create a successfully layered space, believes interior designer Nicola Mardas. 'Part of creating harmony among different design styles is knowing that each piece resonates, that everything holds meaning. The light will almost always be different when travelling, which impacts a culture's colour palette and saturation. A piece that fits in perfectly with the style of that country will likely look very different in your home.' Items like fabric, art or ceramics are relatively simple to integrate into an existing style. 'If a room already contains antiques, it's usually easier to incorporate handcrafted furniture from different parts of the world. However, if there is a more minimalist aesthetic, each new piece you add will stand out more, so careful selection is key.'

WONDERS OF WALLPAPER In the context of decorative arts, wallcoverings are relatively new – in as much as they are a decor, which is printed or painted off-site and installed into a room. The idea, however, of decorating walls with patterns to enhance one's home goes back centuries. 'There has always been an appetite to enhance the beauty of our immediate surroundings, by applying motifs, geometric patterns, painted landscapes, flora and fauna to them,' says Lizzie Deshayes, co-founder of Fromental. 'A room so decorated, with wallpaper, is utterly changed, to express the owner's personality, bring a sense of joy, peace or simply to delight the eye and the heart.'

THE ART OF COLLECTING 'Unique trinkets and objets d'art from far-flung destinations also make up some of our most valuable possessions,' says Martin Waller, founder of Andrew Martin. 'Rather than being limited to one style, now people are influenced by the global assortment of design: from the perfect symmetry of the American look, the magic of African artistry, the serenity of Scandinavia, the heritage of French sophistication and the individualism of British decor.' For this reason, he has coined the current decade the 'kaleidoscope era' – a menagerie of objects laden with nostalgia and sentimentality, each with a truly transporting power. 'Anything goes,' he says, 'and the more unexpected, the better, much like jewellery or cufflinks to an outfit.'

> "When I think about things I've bought on my travels, they transport me back to that place and moment in time"
>
> **SARAH PEAKE**, founder of Studio Peake

The sourcebook: European style

FRENCH BEDROOM
This is an award-winning French furniture boutique founded by Georgia Metcalfe, selling a variety of beds, bed linen, lighting and accessories highlighting the very best in French design.

RIMADESIO
Wigmore Street-based store offering contemporary Italian design turned into bespoke furniture solutions and functional space divisions such as doors, sliding panels, shelving units and walk-in wardrobes.

SCHMIDT
Regarded as the leading French kitchen brand and number one exporter of French kitchen furniture, the company designs made-to-measure pieces for kitchens, bedrooms and living rooms.

FLORIM
For over 60 years, this company, based in the ceramic district of Sassuolo near Modena in Italy, has had a reputation for producing contemporary porcelain stoneware tiles and slabs.

CONTINENTAL CHARACTER

Designer Laura Gonzalez on the appeal of the unique aesthetic European style delivers

CREATING a chic space can often feel quite hard to do – and add a lot of pressure. The most important element to a space is the soul that you bring it. Your home is more than just a showroom.

■ Travelling really informs design. I travel all over Europe, but Paris is always a great source of inspiration. In my opinion, Italy and France are the most important places to discover interesting references. Another place is London, it is also a great inspiration with such a good soul, very chic and timeless with a twist of the unexpected and fun.

■ European style is so desired because it is unique; it has a heritage and history filled with cultural references. As a result, it brings gravitas to a home. I find my inspiration everywhere, from books, cinema, pictures, museums, art, nature, architecture – it can be anything.

■ Incorporating craftsmanship into a room is important: it allows you to include very high-end and refined detailing in a space and create something that's unique. As Europeans, we have some of the best in the world – it draws on our shared history. The key is to create a subtle balance between the refinement of the past and the purity of contemporary forms.

■ Fabric can transform a room. If I just change the fabric on furniture, it brings a new life to the piece. It's the easiest way to make something feel new.

■ It's important to find balance, for example between light and dark. There's no right colour to use – that's a very personal decision – but right now brown is very 'in' and looks very chic. Sumptuous chocolate tones make a space feel wonderfully warm. But even though I like the colour, I'm less keen when it's used all over – I prefer to add a twist and pair with something like a navy blue. I think the combination is so chic. For example, at the gallery, we mixed those two colours with a very light coral to bring some femininity and it works so well.

■ Lighting can totally change the space and it can allow it to adapt depending on the natural light available. When considering lighting, always choose indirect light and the smallest lighting feature you can allow – and never, ever get a strip light.

■ Antiques always bring something special. When I go to a flea market it's the same feeling as when you are a kid and you're looking for a toy to put in your basket: total joy. It's so precious to be able to give new life and a new home to old pieces.

■ Art helps elevate a room and deliver a sense of personality and style. I like to start with the art and envision the rest of the room around it. I've done this in my own gallery: using a Chinese ink painting by Pietro Ruffo and a collage of textiles on wood using resin in a gold shade by the artist Maurizio Donzelli.

■ When you select your furniture, I think the most important thing is to find a balance. But also, to mix it up: we never do matching sofa and armchairs, and we also like to pair antiques with newer pieces (often that we design ourselves).

■ Lighting at night is another moment that you need to think about – focus on the atmosphere you want to create. You want it to feel warm and cosy, so consider fabric shades, and be specific with the warmth in the colour of the bulbs. 🖋

Stockists

Fabrics are so important in my projects: I've always been strongly influenced by Pierre Frey fabric (I had it in my childhood bedroom) – I love the creativity with no boundaries of pattern or colour. I also love Jennifer Shorto fabrics. For lighting, it's always about mixing styles and designs. I like Himawari for contemporary designs and Noguchi – which is, for me, one of the most poetic lights in the world. I design my own furniture, such as the Mawu chair, which I covered in a Jennifer Shorto silk fabric, and the Fuji sofa, where we worked with Pierre Frey to develop a new texture – a flexible mohair and velvet that makes it very luxurious.

FEATURE JESSICA SALTER PHOTOGRAPHS (TOP LEFT AND BOTTOM RIGHT) ©JÉRÔME GALLAND; (TOP RIGHT) © INÈS SILVA SÁ; (BOTTOM LEFT) © STEPHAN JULLIARD

Balance is important, but doesn't need to be symmetrical, as in the pairing of the urn and ceramic vase placed on the table here

A big piece of art helps elevate a room and bring a sense of personality – you can use it as the starting point for decor

Never do matching sofa and chairs: instead create harmony in pattern and colour choices to tie the room together

Lighting creates different focal points; this free-standing lamp is a sculptural piece in its own right, as well as illuminating the sofa

STRACHAN
THE ART OF FINE FURNITURE

SPRING SAVINGS

Luxury bespoke fitted furniture designed just for you

NEW FINISHES | FREE DESIGN PLANNING & FITTING | BUY NOW PAY IN 2026 | 10-YEAR GUARANTEE

With **substantial savings** across our entire collection, now is the perfect opportunity to transform your home and invest in Strachan luxury fitted furniture. Our wide range of designs include everything from bespoke bedrooms and walk-in wardrobes to hardworking home offices, elegant lounges and indulgent dressing rooms. So whatever your vision may be, our expert designers will help you realise it to perfection.

Call today for a copy of our latest brochure or to arrange your **FREE** design consultation.

0800 0138 139

Please quote offer code **HOG250401**, lines open 7 days a week.

www.strachan.co.uk/hog

BEDROOMS | DRESSING ROOMS | WALK-IN WARDROBES | WALL BEDS | STUDIES | LOUNGES | CINEMAS | LIBRARIES

THE JOY OF...

CREATIVE VISION

This month, interior designer Joy Moyler shares the benefits of making a mood board to help a space come to life

Joy is a US-based designer but her work takes her all over the world. Now running her own studio – Joy Moyler Interiors – she has over 25 years of experience and a degree in architecture. She is celebrated for her use of colour and pattern.

" For me, there are two important initial steps for designing a home, hospitality or commercial project. The first step for any client presentation is the mood board. It is the vessel for development of the palette and finishes later. It occurs in the 'concept phase'.

Mood boards are done following initial chats with a client. This is an early marker to check we are on the right track. As the kids would say... "that we understand the assignment". I'm listening intently to the content of the conversation. Particularly their vocal inflections, reading the excitement as they describe past travels, textures, things that really move them. I ask about their relationship to colour and how it influences their life. What kind of positive life experiences they have held on to. Even more, the kinds of rooms these experiences took place in. Anything that is reflected with glee, that makes them feel good generally is most often revealed during this first conversation.

The mood board is really about establishing the essence of what we will see later. I want a client to look at the mood board and *feel* the room before the first coat of paint has been applied. It gets them thinking, but even more it gets them feeling.

I am listening to the description about the first flowers the husband gifted his wife. How they are presented annually as a ritual. How they continue to make her fall in love with him. I am trying to recapture the strength of those emotions in my mood boards. I also want to hear details about their first date. For example, about the silver bracelet the wife was wearing that really caught the husband's eye... how a suggestion of its design may become a curtain tie-back. The kind of cufflinks the husband was wearing when he first held her hand across the table. Maybe it was a rich green enamel finish that can be interpreted into hardware in his dressing room. Those kinds of details – the sentimental sort – is of immense interest. These details are what I want the mood board to relive.

The second step is the palette presentation, what I often refer to as 'second base' of the mood board. It is where the overall palette begins to be defined. This launches the 'schematic design' phase. The real-time introduction of what each of the spaces will look like. How they're going to feel, what special finishes might be in each room. How fabrics will interact and play off of each other. That is the development of the palette. While a particular presentation board or tray will be dedicated to each room or area, we typically only create one mood board for overall project expression. And with that, we often give the mood board to the client before advancing to the next phase of the assignment. With that, we collect our A+ grade! " ©

"I want a client to look at the mood board and *feel* the room before the first coat of paint has been applied"

Mood boards help to refine a project's style

PHOTOGRAPH JAN BALDWIN STYLIST KATRIN CARGILL

LOVE YOUR HOME

SOFAS · ARMCHAIRS · BEDS

www.love-your-home.co.uk

Homes

INSPIRATIONAL INTERIORS FROM TOWN TO COUNTRY

Interior designer Wendy Labrum brought a modern-classic aesthetic to a historic home just outside Chicago (page 104). Painting by Jared Green. Coffee table and sofa designed by Wendy Labrum Interiors. Vintage Knoll Platner chair. Vintage side table and lamp, 1stDibs. Rug, The Rug Company

&

Whether it's the early 19th-century estate in Shropshire or the Parisian abode brimming with personality, each house this month has distinctive style

Under the Tuscan sun

The dappled light streaming through the windows of this Italian farmhouse was hugely influential in all the decorating decisions designer Nicola Harding took when reinventing the property as a luxurious retreat

WORDS FIONA MCCARTHY **PHOTOGRAPHY** WILLIAM JESS LAIRD

ENTRANCE HALL
This provides 'a calming
transition between the
house and garden, and
between the different
rooms,' says Nicola.
Walls in Pure & Original
Silver Clay Fresco. Victorian
library table, Tinker & Toad.
Medici **sconce**, Atelier
Vime Editions. Plaster
cone **light**, Rose Uniacke.
Painting by Christy Matson

SITTING ROOM
'It was important for this space to feel cosy if it is just the husband and wife at home, but with plenty of seating for when people visit,' says Nicola. **Walls in** Pure & Original Calm Fresco. Rattan **chairs**, clients' own; **cushions in** Bhuji in Denim, Namay Samay. Custom Studio **sofa** in heavyweight linen in Clay; seat in Stripe III, Rose Uniacke. Antique white **table lamp and shade**, Caroline de Kerangal. Celadon blue **table lamp** with Robert Kime Papyrus lampshade. **Drapery in** textured linen in Cameo, Rose Uniacke. Antique mahogany **side table**, Miles Griffiths Antiques

EXTERIOR
Intimate spaces under the
shade of the wraparound
terrace are perfect for
enjoying the garden and
olive grove views.
For similar **loungers**
try Neptune

How do you find a compromise between the tastes of an Italian husband and an American wife when bringing an ancient Tuscan farmhouse to life? Bring in the colour- and comfort-loving British interior designer Nicola Harding. 'They wanted something soulful, warm and friendly,' says the designer renowned for her gentle, soothing approach to interiors. 'They wanted a house that would feel immediately like home the minute they arrived, and somewhere relaxing to spend time together as a family and entertain friends.'

The couple, having met 'in some far-flung corner of the world in their twenties and made their fortune in New York from nothing,' says Nicola, bought the house and surrounding olive groves, not far from where he grew up. They wanted to instil in it an element of future-proofing – should their twenty-something children bring friends or start to have families of their own – as well as allowing for the wife to feel at ease having people in her space. 'She was open about finding this difficult, so we needed to make this comfortable for her.'

Nicola's answer was to concentrate on the heart of the house, designing rooms that included an intimate dining room and easy-going living spaces such as a kitchen, sitting room and snug downstairs, as well as four bedrooms and bathrooms upstairs. Outside, a pool house – with a kitchen (doubling as a bar), dining and living areas – was created from scratch and outbuildings were converted into guest cottages, one with its own kitchen and sitting room, affording both the family and guests the perfect balance of privacy and conviviality.

Hard finishes were reused where possible, from the stairs and tiled floors ('much nicer to cover them with really big rugs') and metalwork ('rubbed down and repainted') to asking the builder to give a less than attractive fireplace a sculptural lift in brick and plaster. 'Sometimes, reusing things pushes you to find creative solutions that work better for everyone.'

A bigger main bathroom was also fashioned by removing the walls of a toilet cubicle installed by the previous owners; a butler's pantry was created next to the kitchen and Nicola arranged the basement to include a wine cellar, space for a billiard table and plentiful storage so the house never feels too cluttered.

The designer accentuated the flow of light by 'dialling the colour palette up and down according to the location of each room,' she says, bouncing off the views of olive groves outside. In the darker dining room, shaded by the vine-strewn terrace outside, she swathed the ceiling in red and the walls with a teal blue grasscloth. 'Layering darker colours in different tones from the same family ensures the effect doesn't feel too hectic.' By contrast, in the light-filled sitting room, Nicola layered shades of white with hints of blue in the textiles and lamp bases. 'Blue is such an easy colour to live with,' she says.

It is now a home that feels 'smart and grown up but also welcoming and approachable,' says Nicola. This owes much to the designer's love for seeking out local craftspeople to bring every space 'depth and a sense of history'. Here, artisans have helped with the textural fresco wall finish – 'it really accentuates the dappled light coming through' – to tiling, joinery and rattan work.

She also worked with makers, including Matthew Cox for the dining table, Rose Uniacke for sofas, lighting and linens and Soane Britain for rattan, lights and fabric. 'It's like matchmaking, finding things with interesting stories, be they antiques or new pieces, that resonate with the people who are going to live in the house,' says Nicola. 'That sense of affinity and connection with a piece and the person who made it is what makes someone feel completely at home from the get-go.'

■ nicolaharding.com

"The greatest compliment someone can give me is that it isn't immediately obvious a designer had been involved"

DINING ROOM
Rich colour and texture deliver a sense of depth.
Socle **table**, Matthew Cox.
Chair cushions in Gorjon, Namay Samay. **Ceiling in** Georgetown, Paint & Paper Library. Extra Fine Arrowroot **wallcovering** in Tourmaline, Phillip Jeffries. **Pendant**, Soane Britain. **Lamp**, Tyson London. **Rug**, Tatiana Tafur

SNUG
'I wanted this space to completely envelop the family,' says Nicola.
Walls in Courtly Rose, Pure & Original. **Wall light**, Pinch. **Lamp**, Julian Chichester; bespoke **lampshade** in Anemone paper by Rosi de Ruig. **Sofa** and **ottoman**, both bespoke

"I personally don't feel very at ease when things are too perfect – I think it is imperfection that makes a home comfortable"

KITCHEN
The red island 'gives the room a warm heart and draws the focus to the centre,' says Nicola. **Lower units in** Spruce, Paint & Paper Library; **wall units in** Silver Clay; **island in** Old Wine, both Pure & Original. Camembert **stool**, Howe. Zellige **tiles**, Mosaic Factory. **Pendant lights**, NPage Studio

BEDROOM
This space is in the guest cottage. **Headboard**, KLS Interiors; covered in Christopher Farr Cloth's Echo in Pale Blue. **Walls in** Pure & Original Skin Powder. **Bedspread**, Toast

MAIN BEDROOM
An anteroom leading from here affords the owners a sanctuary. Daisy **pendant; wall light**, both Soane Britain. **Cushion in** woven silk velvet ikat from Nushka

MAIN BATHROOM
Inset shower panelling made from local Breccia Violetta marble lends a jolt of energy. **Walls in** Chalk White by Pure & Original. Zellige **tiles** in colour 1019, Mosaic Factory

MAIN BATHROOM
Pink feet add a playful modern twist to the traditional bath. Rockwell **bath** with feet in pink, The Water Monopoly. **Vanity in** Moorland by Pure & Original. **Wall light**, Collier Webb

CLOAKROOM
This cocooning space, rich in colour and pattern, sits 'somewhere between romance and glamour,' says Nicola. Bespoke **vanity** made locally in Verde Guatemala marble. **Mirror**, Lorfords Antiques. Hopper **wall lights**, Jamb. Palampore Blossom **wallpaper** in Pink and Red, Soane Britain. **Door in** Georgetown, Paint & Paper Library

COURTYARD
Paint for the facade was custom mixed by Pure & Original with shutters in Ethereal Blue by Edward Bulmer Natural Paint. Antique **stool**, Vinterior; covered in Canal Stripe by Perennials Fabrics

EXTERIOR
It was important that the garden flowed around the house. The star jasmine planting 'has the most incredible scent and is clipped to the shape of the windows to feel very architectural,' says Nicola

Q*&*A Nicola Harding
The designer shares her style inspiration

SMALL CHANGE, BIG IMPACT We changed several of the openings from squared tops to rounded, which despite being simple and relatively inexpensive made an enormous impact on leading the eye through the space and how the light flows from one place to another.

YOUR STYLE IN THREE WORDS Soulful, curious, user-friendly.

GO-TO COLOUR Pink. It's nurturing and calming and works at all times of the day, all year. I'll never forget someone telling me that prison cell walls painted pink help to calm the inhabitants.

PLAIN OR PATTERNED... I would rarely do a patterned sofa, it would be more like a patterned accent – the punctuation rather than the main event.

DESCRIBE YOUR DESIGN PROCESS I start with a feeling. I have long conversations with clients about how they want the space to feel, how they want to use it and then the colour palette comes from that because it plays such a big part for me in creating the right mood. Next comes the furniture and lighting; and then fabrics come last.

ENTERTAINING AREA
Everything is completely weatherproof in this space, which is open to the elements all year. **Coffee table** is bepoke; made by a travertine supplier. Atzompa **pendants**, L'Aviva Home

OUTDOOR KITCHEN
Fashioned in steel stainless
and local hardwood, this
is the perfect space for
cooking for large numbers
when entertaining family
and friends.
Splashback in zellige
tiles; for similar try Bert
& May. Salsa **bar stools**,
Sika-Design. Sugar Cone
pendant lights by Rich
Miller from The New
Craftmaker. Travertine
floor tiles sourced locally

DINING ROOM
A digitally printed
reproduction of a
tapestry provides a
cosseting backdrop.
Digitally printed tapestry
wallcovering, a
reproduction of *Triumph
of the Gods* at Dumfries
House, Zardi & Zardi.
Mahogany **commode**,
Geoffrey Stead.
Candelabra, Julia Boston
Antiques. **Wall light**,
Robin Martin Antiques

WE WANTED TO CREATE A HOME THAT FOLDS YOU INTO ITS EMBRACE – IT'S ALL ABOUT ESCAPISM & EXUBERANCE

Celebrating English country house style – from swags and tails to rich damasks – this confident renovation by Guy Goodfellow marries tradition and modern-day comfort

WORDS EMMA J PAGE **PHOTOGRAPHY** ASTRID TEMPLIER

DINING ROOM
'This has seen so many memorable lunches and suppers,' says Guy. 'A chandelier adds grandeur, countered by the simplicity of the rug.' Design GII-03 sisal and hemp **rug**, Alton-Brooke. **Chair seats in** Rigoletto Velvet in Peat, Kerry Joyce; **chair backs in** Hintlesham in Tomato, Guy Goodfellow Collection. George II **mirror**, circa 1740, Edward Hurst. **Fireplace**, Jamb

DINING ROOM
Guy finished doors in faux bois to create a rich mahogany effect. 'I like that there are lots of through-views in the house,' he says. 'It lends a sense of cosiness.' **Curtains in** Harris in Red Earth, Susanna Davis; **lining in** Howe's Lattice in Old Stone. Oak painted and gilded **curtain pole**, David Bedale. Scagliola **column**, Max Rollitt. Cast **bronze bust** of Plato on breccia marble, Guinevere

LIBRARY
Guy rebuilt and regilded the pelmet to allow for more generous curtains. Lammertin **wallpaper** in Malachite, Guy Goodfellow Collection. **Rug**, Tim Page Carpets. Custom Alexandra **sofa** in Jasper Fabrics' Grace-Willow, Michael S Smith. Custom **ottoman in** Fermoie's Satchel. Mahogany **side table**, Sotheby's

Some homes make the heart beat faster thanks to experimental finishes and trend-led schemes, others reveal their treasures more slowly, offering a familiarity that is both comfortable and comforting. This home, part of a country estate in Shropshire, falls into the latter category. A grand entrance, imposing architectural lines, a sweeping staircase and back corridors leading to hidden nooks all conjure a bygone sensibility and yet, in the hands of interior designer Guy Goodfellow, every element has been gently reappraised for modern life.

'For me, a successful country house has to feel authentic and unpretentious rather than overwhelming,' says Guy, who worked on this project for four years. 'That means embracing the melting pot nature of classic English decoration, where "pristine" sits comfortably with "faded around the edges" and furniture is always a little mismatched.'

When Guy started work on the building, designed in 1814 by architect John Hiram Haycock, its interiors did not live up to their setting. His client, who lives here with her grown-up son and frequently has a house full of guests, wanted to honour the English country house aesthetic that she had so long admired. 'She has roots in Germany and Denmark, but she is a self-proclaimed Anglophile,' he explains. 'The idea was to enhance that classic appeal, in many ways returning the house to what it once would have been – a place for friends and guests to gather – minus any feeling of stuffiness, or for that matter, unpredictable bathroom plumbing.'

Known for his attention to detail and his maximalist aesthetic, Guy is adept at making changes so subtle as to be near impossible to track. 'I have an obsession with old houses,' he admits, 'but that doesn't mean you shouldn't alter and adapt. In this case, we moved the kitchen to a sunny extension and carved out space for the kind of bathrooms I love – ones that feel more like furnished rooms than utilitarian spaces.'

That approach extends throughout this house, where antique finds sit alongside original period details and blowsy floral prints rub shoulders with wall murals in rich ochres, chocolates and tobaccos. If they look as if they've been there forever, then all the better, according to Guy, though in reality many of these elements have been recently introduced. The dining room walls are hung with a digitally reproduced copy of a series of tapestries at Dumfries House called *Triumph of the Gods*, with technology allowing the borders to be adjusted to frame each wall exactly. Deeply tactile, the finish instantly humanises these grand proportions.

In the entrance hall, Guy refinished white columns in a rich oxide red to simulate porphyry, while doors throughout have been treated with a faux bois painted effect. The library bookcases were taken apart and rebuilt more generously, while original pelmet boards were restructured, regilded and replaced to carry more generous curtains. Even the stainless-steel island counter in the kitchen has an invisible heating mechanism to keep plates warm.

'The best part was our excitement at finding just the right piece,' reflects Guy. 'We spent many happy mornings with our client at various antiques fairs. One day, we found an oak curtain pole, with gilded brackets and finials, that fitted the dining room window perfectly without any alteration – that was a lovely moment.'

It's for this reason perhaps that the renovation meandered through the years, with the resulting sense that the schemes in this home have evolved organically. And for Guy, that's the epitome of a successful country house. 'You want to come home from a damp walk with the spaniel to a roaring open fire and a hint of wood smoke,' he says. 'It's about gathering your nearest and dearest within exuberant rooms that spark conversation and fun.' If that's the code for happy country living, it looks like this home has cracked it.

■ guygoodfellow.com

"Every room is zoned so its proportions don't feel formidable – there are cosy banquettes here and snug work spots there"

KITCHEN
Two large tables were replaced with banquettes to fit a crowd.
Banquettes in Twelve Bar Stripe in Sage, Sand & Wine, GP & J Baker.
Dining chairs, Guy Goodfellow Collection.
Pendant, Soane Britain

KITCHEN
The island top has a heating mechanism to keep hot buffets warm.
Kitchen by Cleary & Hall, with Lacanche range. Custom hand-painted Alcazar splashback **tiles** with border detail, Douglas Watson Studio

5 rules of
CLASSIC ENGLISH STYLE
Guy Goodfellow shares his design advice

1. Rather than relying on three or four bright bulbs, amp it up to 10 but dim them down – it gives you a much softer reflected light.

2. English style is always a melting pot, with furniture and objects collected from around the world. If each object is of merit and beauty, they will complement one another.

3. Play with scale – for example, apply architectural balance to a furniture layout to echo a room's proportions and then break that symmetry with a single piece that feels off-kilter or slightly unbalanced. It adds a little humour.

4. Consider more than just the interior – think about the context too, starting with the view from the main gate, the approach, the landscape.

5. Country life calls for different priorities: a focus on practicalities and slower, more comfortable elements. Sink-in armchairs, fireplaces and boot rooms take the place of slicker, more refined, urban elements.

KITCHEN COURTYARD

Modelled on the outdoor space at members' club 5 Hertford Street, this is wired for sound and fitted with awnings for all-weather gatherings. Design and structure, I & J Bannerman. **Tables**, Hervé Baume. **Chairs**, Collier Webb. **Cushions** and **slipcovers** in York Stripe, Fermoie.

BEDROOM
This playful scheme features tent storage in smart ticking. Trumeau **mirror**, Kate Thurlow. **Walls in** English Toile fabric in Pale Blue on Oyster, Bennison. Tented **wardrobe in** Ian Mankin's Ticking Stripe 1 in Airforce. Louis XVI fruitwood and inlaid marble top **commode**, Hugh Leuchars

MAIN BEDROOM
A pear-shaped mirror adds a softening touch. **Curtains** and **bed canopy in** Bennison's Palampore in Original on Oyster. **Window seat** (at foot of bed), Wakelin & Linfield; upholstered in Pierre Frey's Dolino in Galet

BEDROOM
'We had fun decorating every bedroom individually, from abundant florals to textured plains,' says Guy. **Headboard and valance in** Temple in Lilac, Veere Grenney. George III **table**, Windsor House Antiques

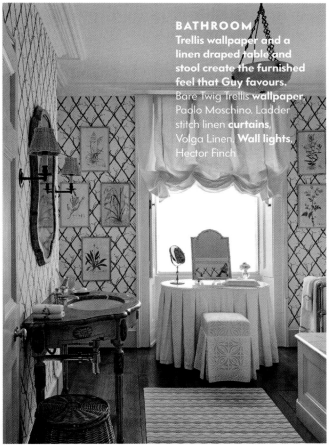

BATHROOM
Trellis wallpaper and a linen draped table and stool create the furnished feel that Guy favours. Bare Twig Trellis **wallpaper**, Paolo Moschino. Ladder stitch linen **curtains**, Volga Linen. **Wall lights**, Hector Finch

SITTING ROOM
The custom joinery has been painted in the same earthy red as the walls for a cocooning feel. **Walls and joinery in** Masai by Paint & Paper Library. **Curtains in** Hamac sheer by Métaphores

Set the mood

Coaxing this Victorian property into the 21st century, Tom Morris of Morrisstudio has crafted contemporary schemes where rich colours play a starring role

WORDS VIVIENNE AYERS **PHOTOGRAPHY** BOZ GAGOVSKI

SITTING ROOM
A green sofa injects
energy. Tom added navy
blue piping that links to
the Japanese boro cloth
artwork and cushions.
Bespoke **sofa in** Old Flax in
Catalpa Green by Soane
Britain, with **trim** by Houlès.
Pendant, vintage. **Rug**,
Jaipur Rugs. **Cushions**,
Lola & Mawu. Japanese
boro cloth **artwork**, Sauce

DINING AREA
The early-20th-century anthropological prints were spotted by Tom a few years ago. 'They're really beautiful and this was the perfect spot for them,' he says.
Prints, Quindry. 1950s teak and oak **chairs** from Chase & Sorensen. **Table and runner**, client's own. **Curtain in** Fil-à-Fil by Inga Sempé for Kvadrat. **Artwork**, Ashoka panel by Robert Kime. **Walls in** Hawkesmoor, Mylands

Behind the facade of this classic three-storey Victorian property in London lies a completely unexpected interior. Alluring use of colour, rich woods, crafted furniture and beguiling fabrics inject a certain joie de vivre that ensures the interior sings. It's a quintessential design by Tom Morris of Morrisstudio, who describes his signature style as 'steering towards earthy or warmer tones, a touch more on the masculine side but never too overdesigned or stylised, with a diverse mix of things'.

The brief from the client, who had lived in the house for some time, was to make the interior more cohesive and improve storage. Tom's solution involved devising a colour scheme that brought everything together, utilising the space with custom joinery and elevating the interior with bespoke pieces and Danish furniture.

Colour was woven through in a way that infuses a sense of modernity. In the punchy sitting room, for instance, the palette was inspired by the work of artist Frank Auerbach, resulting in an ode to colour. 'We really wanted to bring in some lovely warm earth tones,' says Tom. 'Frank would have quite a moody, dark colour palette and against it there would be brighter colours, so that's why we brought in a bespoke pistachio green sofa, as well as all the indigo shades.'

The clients were keen to incorporate more storage and Tom introduced custom joinery that is painted in the same earthy red hue as the walls. Sitting neatly in alcoves on either side of the sitting room fireplace, the cabinetry provides practical storage, as well as a handy drinks cabinet. Rich wooden detailing injects extra depth. 'I was trying to create something useful, but also make a feature of it,' says Tom. 'We added the ply background to link to the original floorboards, which have been beautifully treated, so it's a way of mirroring them as well.' The chestnut tone of a Josef Hoffmann chair works beautifully in the mix, while a sleek leather chair is another iconic vintage Danish piece. 'I was trying to do a lot with a little so that each piece worked cohesively as a whole, while still keeping the room fairly open,' says Tom. In keeping with his ethos of not overdesigning, he chose a simple but effective sheer fabric at the window to provide privacy. 'Light filters through it and it has the most beautiful dappled texture,' he reveals. Japanese boro cloth artwork, cushions and an Indian rug infuse pops of indigo and evoke an eclectic feel.

The blue and red colour scheme was then teased through into the next-door kitchen where it translates as a paler blue and pink. 'We chose the colours to contrast with the sitting room, where we've gone for the reds in one room, it's pinks in the kitchen,' explains Tom. 'I was very conscious of the kitchen clashing with the sitting room, so the bases are quite complementary.' Statement fabrics, such as the striped curtains and blinds, catch the eye, while an exquisite fabric by Robert Kime was framed and made into an artwork. The dark wood kitchen cabinetry, which already existed, links with the walnut timber in the sitting room, while the thread of iconic Danish design is continued with the mid-century Chase & Sorensen dining chairs.

The large Victorian house is notable for its good proportions. However, Tom faced a challenge on the first floor, where an open-plan layout meant that the client could see from the bedroom through to the bathroom beyond. Stud walling was therefore installed and the door moved to provide a grander entrance to the space, and the bed was repositioned to sit on the fireplace wall and joinery installed either side, improving the sight lines through to the bathroom. Tom then created a dressing room space with mirrors on the cupboard doors to bring in light and incorporated double-sided fabric curtains to close off the bedroom, dressing room and bathroom when necessary. 'It was a way of making a focal point of the opening yet softening it, and using colour to section out each space without being too out of sync with each other,' he says.

The house's grand scale ensures that the interior feels quite contemporary, which fed into Tom's design narrative. As he concludes: 'The interior space allowed us to blend different styles and different periods to create something truly singular.' ⊗

■ morrisstudio.co.uk

DRESSING AREA
Curtains separate this space from the bedroom and bathroom. 'We made a feature of them with double-sided fabric,' explains Tom.
Curtains in Burnley Ticking (using two different colours back to back), Howe at 36 Bourne Street. Grasscloth **wallcovering**, Nobilis

EN SUITE
This soothing green space is Tom's favourite room. 'The bath is vast and sits under a bright window,' he says. 'It's the most lovely calm place.'
Rockwell **bath**, The Water Monopoly. Kelly **floor lamp**, Porta Romana. **Blind in** Primrose linen by Volga. Lyon limestone **floor tiles**, Mandarin Stone. **Walls in** Wattle V by Paint & Paper Library

Q*&*A Tom Morris
The designer shares his style inspiration

BIGGEST INDULGENCE The Rockwell bath from The Water Monopoly. Grand enough for two!

SMALL CHANGE, BIG IMPACT An internal curtain really helps seal off the occasionally too-grand grandeur of Victorian proportions.

GO-TO COLOUR Masai by Paint & Paper Library has a lovely chalky depth to it that is low on pigment, so it can read as a soft brown in some lights, then a proper red when light hits it.

FAVOURITE DESIGNER/BRAND Kvadrat I go to again and again for textiles. Santa & Cole for lighting.

DESIGN HERO Oscar Niemeyer.

INSPIRATION Books, travel, the inner recesses of a very complex brain.

SECRET ADDRESS Duncan Clarke at Adire African Textiles at Alfies Antique Market is a bank of information when it comes to African textiles and somewhere I go for the final elements of a room.

MAIN BEDROOM
The Indian carving was left by the previous owners. Tom restored it and made a feature of it, hanging it up above the bed to crown it. Zettel'z **pendant** by Ingo Maurer. **Curtains in** Laundered linen by Warwick. **Quilt**, Yoruba indigo cloths by Adire African Textiles. **Headboard and cushion in** Obernai jacquard, Pierre Frey. Grand **rug** in Moss by Nordic Knots

SITTING ROOM
Maintaining the building's original character was key to the renovation, and here wooden beams, a large fireplace and traditional panelling sit comfortably with modern floor-to-ceiling glazing. **Curtains in** linen from Nobilis. Bespoke **sofas** (near window) designed by Wendy Labrum Interiors in shearling from Edelman. **Pendants**, Rose Uniacke

MAKING HISTORY

In a historic home in a Chicago suburb, designer
Wendy Labrum deftly honoured the house's
past while weaving in modern elements

WORDS JULIET BENNING **STYLING** DARWIN FITZ **PHOTOGRAPHY** AIMÉE MAZZENGA/JBSA

reservation isn't high on the agenda in Hinsdale, a western suburb of Chicago. In fact, many old homes are getting knocked down in favour of new builds. So when interior designer Wendy Labrum was asked to redesign her clients' recently acquired historic home, she was eager to lend her expertise. 'When Chicago was first built, this was a neighbourhood of old money, which is why there are so many beautiful mansions. But rather than take these on, a lot of people are opting to build generic and big boxy new properties,' says Wendy. 'My clients had the budget to build something new and fancy, but it's not what they wanted. They were keen to take something much older and do a period-appropriate and sensitive renovation. This approach can actually be more challenging, though, as the city can make you jump through more hoops.'

The house the couple had settled on was built in 1926 and combines details from the American Craftsman period with some Georgian elements. 'The architecture is a bit of a hybrid and when we did the renovation we brought in American and English inspiration. We looked at Monticello in Virginia, which was Thomas Jefferson's home, as a point of reference,' Wendy explains. Continuity was another important factor. 'My clients wanted any development to be true to the house's origins. We went to great lengths to source specific bricks that would match what was there.' Also on-board as architect was Michael Abraham, who knew the house well, having provided drawings for an earlier renovation of the property some 30 years back.

'The owners had bought the house from an older couple who had looked after it well, but with three young children and a dog they felt some adaptations would be needed for modern family life,' Wendy says. The four-year project went in phases, and after buying the plot next door, the couple have created a pool, which is heavily used during Chicago's hot summers.

'The house is now three separate structures inspired by an old English estate,' explains Wendy. 'The original garage was converted into a pool house, with masses of light coming in through steel-framed windows that take up the position of the former garage doors. A new garage was built on the next-door plot.'

The family, who had been living in a smaller property in the same area, brought only their piano with them. 'With furniture and art, we started from scratch. We purchased a lot of antiques and sourced pieces from all over the world. Our clients had discerning taste, but they trusted us to do our work and had no problem visualising our concepts, which made it all feel more seamless,' Wendy says. 'While I often work with an art curator or consultant, I sourced the art for this project myself. As a graduate in art history, I have perspective but not the same breadth of knowledge as a curator. I just wanted the art to add a magical alchemy to the interiors.'

The more formal and subdued rooms favoured by the former owners were reimagined for a high-energy modern family. 'We reconfigured the entryway and took space from the walkway to the old library to create a larger mudroom,' Wendy explains. 'We also transformed an attic wardrobe into a much-needed home office.'

The sloped ceilings and angled walls at the top of the house were a design challenge that she relished. 'We lined the office walls with striped fabric using a pattern-drench idea to make it cosy and special,' Wendy says. 'I can't do anything that's 100% traditional, so I always add some kind of contemporary twist. Often this might come from furnishings or light fittings.'

Similarly, in an attic bedroom, Wendy used polished plaster to create a cosseting scheme that embraces the slanting ceiling and roof lines. Design details like these truly work to improve the quirks of the architecture, and can be found throughout the house. The recipient of a huge character injection and masses more functionality, this older generation home has long secured its future. ▣

■ wendylabruminteriors.com

"We wanted to be true to the house's origins – we went to great lengths to secure bricks that would match what was there"

DINING ROOM
Bespoke white oak wall panelling evokes the intimate atmosphere of the former library. The flooring is in custom white oak herringbone. **Chandelier**, Alexandre Logé at 1stDibs. Travertine **table**, Atelier Jouvence Custom Stoneworks. Cab **chairs**, Cassina. **Painting** by Matthias Fabre

KITCHEN-DINER
A mid-century dining table and custom-made light fixture strike an elegant note.
Table, Charlotte Perriand. Saarinen Tulip **chairs**, Knoll. Bespoke **pendant** designed by Wendy Labrum Interiors

Q&A Wendy Labrum

The designer shares her style inspiration

BIGGEST INDULGENCE The owners giving us the freedom to do what was right for the project.

GREATEST SUCCESS The dynamic with my clients.

GO-TO COLOUR A warm kind of rusty red.

YOUR STYLE IN THREE WORDS
Elegant, timeless, comfortable.

DESIGN HERO There are so many, but one is Frances Elkins – she was such a pioneer in the industry and an inspiration for all women in business.

SECRET ADDRESS Off-the-beaten-path antique stores. It's great to develop a relationship with local owners as they can be invaluable sourcing experts.

LAST PIECE OF ART BOUGHT FOR YOUR HOME
A large-scale abstract piece by Andrey Samarin.

MUSEUM YOU VISITED RECENTLY The Hôtel de la Marine in Paris. It's small, but it showcases some of the best historical architecture and details you'll see in the city.

KITCHEN
Calacatta Viola marble makes maximum impact and is offset by the muted tones of the cooker hood, units and Venetian plaster ceiling.
Cabinetry designed by Wendy Labrum Interiors.
Range cooker, Lacanche.
Ceiling lights, Apparatus.
Stools, Rose Uniacke

BANQUETTE
This additional seating area is often used for homework and playing games. Leather offers a practical yet stylish finish for the upholstery.
Walls and **ceiling in** bespoke Venetian plaster.
Blind in fabric from S Harris.
Antique **table**, 1stDibs.
Sculpture by Mirjam de Nijs. **Painting** by Frédéric Heurlier Cimolai

BEDROOM
Sloping ceilings have a tent-like effect that has been emphasised with two different wall finishes. Bespoke **bed** by Wendy Labrum Interiors in a Rose Tarlow fabric. Vintage **pendant**; **table**, both 1stDibs. **Rug**, Armadillo

STUDY
The walls and ceiling have been upholstered to create a characterful and quiet space. **Walls** and **ceiling in** fabric by Kerry Joyce. Vintage table **lamp**, 1stDibs. **Chair**; **desk**, both vintage Göran Malmvall

CLOAKROOM
Brass fittings and a gilt mirror sing out in this warm-neutral scheme. Vintage **sconces**, 1stDibs. **Basin** and **taps**, Kohler. Floor **tiles**, Ann Sacks

EN SUITE
The bath is perfectly positioned to admire the treetops and painting. **Bath, tap** and heated **towel rail**, Waterworks. **Artwork** by Rick Lewis

POOL
The owners bought the plot alongside their own to make space for a pool and a new garage building with a 'she shed' above. **Outdoor furniture**, Janus et Cie. **Grill**, Big Green Egg. **Architecture** by Michael Abraham Architecture

THROUGH THE LOOKING GLASS

Each room in this Parisian family home reveals a different world – and is testament to the vision of its polymath creative and entrepreneur owner Ramdane Touhami

WORDS RACHEL LEEDHAM **PHOTOGRAPHY** ARI

KITCHEN
'I wanted this space to be warm and welcoming but also Mediterranean – which is where I'm from – and with a crafted feel,' notes Ramdane of the aesthetic. The tiles, which were custom made in Umbria, were combined with steel appliances which serve to reflect the terracotta to ensure that it is the star of the show. Appliances, Gaggenau

DINING ROOM
Around the top of the space are the names of people who left their mark on the house, created by Ramdane's own typography studio. **Glass etching** (within the bespoke cupboards), Christian Fournie. **Furniture** made by lacquer artisans

SITTING ROOM
The fireplace is surrounded by tiles featuring tarot cards, a gift to former resident Jean-Claude Carrière from the filmmaker Luis Buñuel. A reproduction of the Kangaroo **chair** by Pierre Jeanneret is by Cassina

SITTING ROOM
Sofa specialists originally deemed Ramdane's designs too complex to make. In the end they found the technical solution and everyone is very proud of the result. For a similar **floor lamp**, try Vinterior

SITTING ROOM
The frames for the vintage Asafo flags are incorporated into the ebony burl panelling. Try Vinterior for an Eros black marble **table** by Angelo Mangiarotti. Adire African Textiles sources vintage **Asafo flags**

Picture the craftsmen's emphatic Gallic shrugs when Ramdane Touhami first presented them with the plans for the drawing room of his family's new home in Paris' 9th Arrondissement. The maverick French-Moroccan designer and entrepreneur, who runs his own creative agency, tasked them with panelling the walls with ebony burl; but the panelling needed to appear to peel away in the corners to reveal traditional mouldings – suggesting another world behind this world. 'It was pretty complex to produce,' acknowledges Ramdane of a process that involved soaking the wood for two months in order to achieve the precise curl he had in mind.

There is nothing mundane about the home Ramdane and his wife, Victoire de Taillac-Touhami – together the couple revived Cire Trudon, the world's oldest candle manufacturer, and relaunched Jean-Vincent Bully, a 19th-century Parisian parfumerie as Officine Universelle Buly – share with their three children, aged between 17 and 22. From the kitchen, tiled head-to-toe in Etruscan-style terracotta, to the dining room, where giant illuminated spiders crawl across the ceiling, every space offers a glimpse into the mind of an irrepressible avant-garde creative. 'I wanted a home where you have the impression of travelling from one room to the next, with a surprise behind each door,' Ramdane explains. The family had been living in an apartment on the Left Bank when they learnt that this house in the Pigalle district was for sale. 'In typical Ramdane style, he had made an offer within two days,' recounts Victoire, who is Buly's brand and image director.

The house is one of a pair facing each other across a courtyard and it is steeped in history: Henri de Toulouse-Lautrec is believed to have rented the top floor when the lower floors were a brothel; the writers Stefan Zweig and Alphonse Allais both spent stints here; and during the art deco period it belonged to an artisanal rug maker who worked with the prestigious designer Émile-Jacques Ruhlmann. Since the late 1970s, the building had been owned by the illustrious screenwriter, novelist and actor Jean-Claude Carrière, who died a year before the couple bought it. 'It was filled with his art collections and books,' Victoire recalls.

Apart from removing a mezzanine level on the uppermost floor, the pair didn't touch the layout, and Victoire was happy to grant her husband free rein with

the interiors. 'This was a chance for us to experience living in Ramdane's imagination,' she says, adding, 'He worked fast, visiting the site morning, noon and night for nine months. He wanted to make every single decision.'

Teams of craftsmen were enlisted, including lacquer artisans who created the glossy furniture and cupboard doors in the dining room, which resembles the glamorous art deco interior of an ocean liner. For the sitting room's low-slung seating – crafted from what appear to be giant felt-covered pipes – Ramdane tracked down talented specialists in the east of France. 'Their first response to his designs was "non", which in French is usually the starting point of the conversation. We never take it personally,' laughs Victoire.

Her favourite space is the kitchen: 'It was difficult for me to understand the design before I saw it but it is stunning; the terracotta gives a special warmth,' she notes. On the lower-ground level is a resistance swimming pool, which Ramdane created for Victoire, a keen swimmer. 'Never in my mind did I imagine that I would have a pool in my basement,' she marvels.

If pieces weren't custom made, they were sourced by Ramdane at auction or from flea markets, and this includes the chic Italian furniture in the couple's bedroom. 'All of us have these tiny, very elegant Italian beds – we live in an aesthetic dictatorship,' quips Victoire, who is quick to point out the benefits of this autocracy: 'We are surrounded by extraordinary things. For example, when you open the cupboards in the dining room, you see this amazing green lacquer. I'm mesmerised by its beauty every time.' 🖼

■ buly1803.com

BEDROOM
When Ramdane and Victoire bought the house, this space was an atelier with a mezzanine level. The plaster mouldings have been painted in a gentle ombré effect. Try Vinterior for D90 **beds** by Carlo de Carli for Sormani

STUDY
'This is Ramdane's sanctuary where everything that is most precious to him goes,' says Victoire. The swimming pool is across the way. **Carpet** designed by Ramdane Touhami

3 rules for
BUYING VINTAGE
Ramdane Touhami shares the secrets of collecting

1. Hone your eye. I have visited Les Puces de Saint-Ouen most weekends for the past 15 years, sourcing pieces for the shops but also for myself. The more you go, and the more you chat with the dealers, the more you understand.

2. Spend time on the websites of lesser-known auction houses. I like small, specialist houses and I like to buy Danish furniture from Denmark, Italian pieces from Italy and so on. My favourite antiques fair is the biannual Mercanteinfiera in Parma.

3. While there is probably a lot to be said for sourcing antiques specifically for a space, this isn't my approach – I tend to collect and then build interiors around the pieces I have collected.

BATHROOM
Ramdane has mixed colourful stones – Blue Bahia granite and Carrara, Rosso Levanto, Verde Guatemala and Rosa Tea marbles – to striking effect. Taps and shower fittings, Atelier Traditionnel du Vimeu. The Invisible Collection sells re-editions of the Satellite **mirror** by Eileen Gray and the **sconce** by Pierre Chareau

Six issues for £6*

May 2023

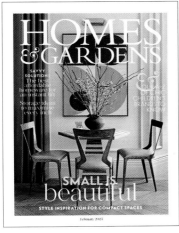

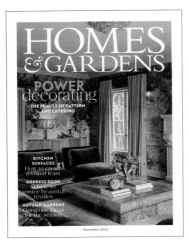

SUBSCRIBER BENEFITS

- Save on the cover price
- Stunning interiors inspiration every month
- Advice from the world's best designers
- Never miss an issue with convenient home delivery
- NEW! Digital access to 120+ issues when you subscribe to print**

TWO EASY WAYS TO SUBSCRIBE

Online at homesandgardenssubs.com/MAY25

or call 0330 333 1113

and quote code DJ38D

Lines open Monday-Friday 8.30am-7pm and Saturday 10am-3pm (UK time)

Bramblecrest®

OUTDOOR DINING | OUTDOOR LIVING | OUTDOOR LOUNGING

Discover our
2025 collections

Gardens
OUTSIDE INTERESTS IN ALL FORMS

Vibrant purple and white agapanthus line a path in this stunning Mallorcan garden nestled in the Tramuntana mountains. See more on page 128

Tour a Mediterranean garden, see how tiling can transform your space, shop our outdoor furniture edit and get ready for the RHS Chelsea Flower Show

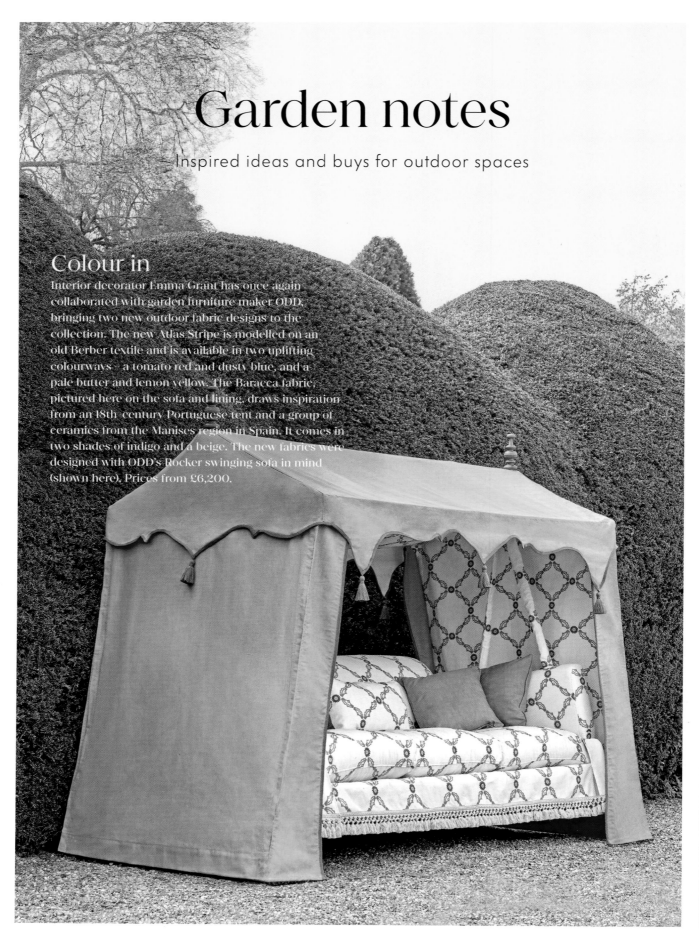

Garden notes

— Inspired ideas and buys for outdoor spaces

Colour in

Interior decorator Emma Grant has once again collaborated with garden furniture maker ODD, bringing two new outdoor fabric designs to the collection. The new Atlas Stripe is modelled on an old Berber textile and is available in two uplifting colourways — a tomato red and dusty blue, and a pale butter and lemon yellow. The Baracca fabric, pictured here on the sofa and lining, draws inspiration from an 18th-century Portuguese tent and a group of ceramics from the Manises region in Spain. It comes in two shades of indigo and a beige. The new fabrics were designed with ODD's Rocker swinging sofa in mind (shown here). Prices from £6,200.

FEATURE HOLLY RANSOME PHOTOGRAPHS (IN THE SHADE) ALEX SUDRON

Hard-working weaves

Christopher Farr Cloth has recently launched five new performance fabrics that offer durability without compromising on style. Calvari Woven, the stripe pictured here, was inspired by the Calvari Steps of Pollença. It's priced at £135m and comes in seven muted colours that have a timeworn feel. Also seen here is the new Inca Velvet inspired by the market town of Inca in the heart of Mallorca. The hard-wearing velvet, priced at £175m, is made from recycled materials and comes in an array of joyful colours such as fuchsia pink and tangerine orange.

CRAFT WORK

For a garden investment that is both beautiful and practical, look to Ferréol Babin's Coucou – one in a series of charming birdhouse sculptures that the French artist carves from wood. Each one is unique and the surface is beautifully shaped with curved undulations created by handcarving. Ferréol works with many types of wood to form a patchwork effect. Prices are available on request.

BEAUTIFUL BASICS

If you feel you may benefit from a reminder to embrace your chores with a spring in your step, this steel utility bucket, from Toast's spring-summer collection A Lightness of Being, is a worthy investment at £30. Ideal for collecting weeds or storing garden tools or cleaning products, the jolly shade of nasturtium red is sure to look pretty in your home and provide an instant mood lift.

In the shade

Plia Parasols has recently launched new frames made from bamboo – a more sustainable choice due to its fast-growing and greenhouse-gas-absorbing qualities. Bamboo's tensile strength is comparable to steel so you don't have to worry about potential damage on windy days. The fabrics are hand-picked to ensure lovely designs that are also hard-wearing. Pictured is the Terracotta scalloped parasol with a cream fringe, £2,195.

Show time

This year's RHS Chelsea Flower Show, taking place from 20-24 May, promises a great line-up inspirational gardens – here are a few highlights

INTELLIGENT GARDENING

Gold-medal-winning designers Tom Massey and Je Ahn return to Chelsea with the Avanade 'Intelligent' Garden, showcasing the role cutting-edge AI technology can play in managing a garden efficiently. An AI assistant will monitor soil moisture, pH values, temperature and rainfall to allow the gardening team to provide precise yet sustainable care. Standout elements will be a pavilion constructed from biodegradable mycelium panels and planting that mimics a natural forest.

GARDEN OF THE FUTURE

The Killik & Co Futureproof Garden by Baz Grainger offers a glimpse of what UK gardens could look like in 25 years. Inspired by the coastal climate of south-west France, Baz's garden is divided into three, with a family space and a water capture area, which directs excess run-off to a pool that flows into a designated flood zone. There is a 3D-printed pergola, and the drought-tolerant planting includes trees such as *Zelkova* and *Pinus mugo*.

PET PARADISE

Gardeners' World's Monty Don has stepped out of his role as a much-loved presenter to design his first Chelsea garden. A celebration of our canine best friends, Monty says the RHS and Radio 2 Dog Garden will offer everything dogs love, while also providing a beautiful space for their owners. A large tree will shade a central lawn, designed for napping dogs, while spring bulbs mingle with longer grasses to create a meadow effect, and a brick path leads to a timber summerhouse where both pooches and people can relax.

ROYAL CONNECTIONS

Gold medallist Joe Perkins returns with The King's Trust Garden: Seeding Success. Reflecting the experiences of the resilient young people the charity supports, it focuses on climate adaptation and pioneering plants. Joe was inspired by volcanic environments, where seeds survive the adverse conditions to deliver new growth. Glass panels depicting seed dispersal methods weave through the space, while recycled and reclaimed materials and naturalistic planting underpin the design.

JEWEL PURPOSE

The Boodles Raindance Garden by Catherine MacDonald celebrates the 25th anniversary of the Raindance jewellery collection, featuring rare coloured gemstones and diamonds. Catherine has designed circular paving pads, etched with concentric circles, that lead to a domed pavilion, which channels rainwater into a sparkling rill. Three platinum-finished water features, arranged in a diamond bezel configuration, complement the predominantly green planting.

PLANTS FOR POSITIVE CHANGE

The Glasshouse Garden, designed by Jo Thompson, will shine a light on the work of The Glasshouse programme, which provides horticultural training to women in prison, providing them with the skills to enter the work world after release. An immersive, reflective space, the garden features a translucent elliptical pavilion emerging from a rich mix of multi-stemmed birch trees, ferns and grasses. *&*

FEATURE ZIA ALLAWAY **PHOTOGRAPHS** (PET PARADISE) RHS/WILLIAM NATHAN

Revive, Reimagine and Refresh with Reupholstery

REUPHOLSTERY · SOFA COVERS · CURTAINS
Sale now on
HURRY · OFFERS END SOON

CLARKE & CLARKE   Sanderson   MORRIS & Cº   WARWICK   EDINBURGH WEAVERS

Breathe new life into your favourite furniture with the craft of reupholstery. From cherished family sofas to beloved heirloom armchairs, our skilled experts carefully strip each piece, restore its frame and interior springs, and bring it back to life in your choice of over 800 stunning fabrics. Combining craftsmanship, sustainability, and timeless style, here at Plumbs, we have been helping homes feel more special for over 60 years—because some things are too valuable to replace.

★ Trustpilot
★★★★★
Rated **Excellent**

Plumbs
Crafted by our family. Loved by yours.

To arrange your free no-obligation home visit, call **01772 83 84 78** quoting **A701 HGA** or visit **plumbs.co.uk** and request our latest brochure.

f ⓘ

Personal retreats

Venture beyond the perfectly presented rooms of leading
interior designers and into their treasured private gardens

Michelle Nussbaumer's garden in San Miguel de Allende, Mexico, features 'outdoor rooms' like this terrace

Veere Grenney's garden in Tangier, Morocco, has a framework of evergreens

FEATURE HOLLY RANSOME PHOTOGRAPHS (LEFT) MAX KIM-BEE, (RIGHT) FRANCESCO LAGNESE

WHEN it comes to creating beautiful things and spaces, many artistic people can turn their hand to any medium. This is the premise of this new book by Dara Caponigro, the creative director of Schumacher. Dara went on a journey to explore what's behind the back door of the homes of the world's leading interior designers, revealing their approach to their gardens and outdoor spaces.

Many apply the same design logic as they would when curating interiors. Emma Burns, joint managing director at Sibyl Colefax & John Fowler, thinks of the garden of her Oxfordshire home 'as a series of rooms that lead from one to the next'. In the outdoor space of the Lourmarin home that belonged to the late decorating icon François Catroux, there is a 'living room' where embedded river stones in a deck echo the pattern of a Moroccan rug. Stephen Sills designed his garden from the inside out, with every window looking onto a carefully arranged still life. For Bunny Williams, it was helpful to tackle the vast openness of her garden by mimicking 'walls' to create intimate zones.

As well as bestowing nuggets of garden design wisdom, this book gives the nosy ones among us the chance to take a closer look at the private worlds of creatives. Carl D'Aquino is all the more interesting now we know he has a penchant for collecting birdhouses, as is Todd Nickey of Nickey Kehoe for revealing his love of the chickens he keeps in his garden in Pasadena.

As Dara points out about people who dedicate their lives to interiors, 'those drawn to the home tend to be grounded and real', and there is something restorative about peeking into the more unruly spaces of these creative people where, unlike indoors, design components cannot be fixed into stillness as the seasons and weather have the upper hand. ⦿

Glorious Gardens: Private Edens of the World's Leading Interior Designers by Dara Caponigro (£54.95, The Monacelli Press and *FREDERIC* magazine) is published on 7 May

Mediterranean
MARVEL

The gardens of this estate in Mallorca, which
include a wildflower meadow and orchard,
are designed to provide interest all year

WORDS ANNETTE WARREN **PHOTOGRAPHY** CLIVE NICHOLS

A stepping-stone gravel path leads to the swimming pool with the new build house beyond

The terrace in front of the house features colourful agapanthus and mounds of Mexican fleabane, *Erigeron karvinskianus*

Waves of clipped
rosemary and domes
of tree germander are
planted in the shady
breakfast area to the
front of the house

ONE OF

the first things I do when I design a garden, is to work out how it will flow,' says Alexander Warren-Gash, lead designer and co-owner of Mashamba Garden Design.

When Alexander was first approached by the owners of a recently completed country estate near Puigpunyent in the Tramuntana mountains of Mallorca, his brief for the garden was very straightforward. ''Keep it simple and romantic' – so in essence I had free rein!' he recalls. Choosing the right plants was key to the design. 'I start with statement trees, then list the medium-sized clipped shrubs before filling in the gaps with smaller plants – the flowers and herbs. Once we have a concept that everyone's happy with, we then make the magic happen! It really was a blank canvas – there was nothing there at all.' The soil on the terraces was imported after the house build; 'I always say it's better to invest in proper ground preparation rather than bigger plants in poor soil.'

The formal gardens are wide, stretching left to right away from the back of the house in a crescent. To one side, the shady dining terrace looks towards a fruit orchard planted with apricot, orange and pomegranate trees. Ribbons of purple lavender lead the eye to the perimeter of the garden. 'We cut the heads off the lavender once it's finished flowering, around June, then we'll cut it back a bit harder in the autumn so it will be looking its best the following year.'

A group of trees screen the villa from the drive. 'I've added pale purple *Tulbaghia violacea* here, which gives a pop of colour beneath the darker trees. Designing this end of the garden in a curve gives the impression that the planting continues around the corner.'

The plants around the pool are deliberately more tropical. *Pittosporum tobira*, AGM (mock Orange), *Cycas revoluta* (Japanese sago palm) and blue agapanthus are key plants. The pots were sourced and planted by Alexander's wife, Jennifer, who specialises in terrace design but the large rectangular concrete planters were Alexander's own creation.

The breakfast area outside the front of the house is an oasis of calm. A central olive tree casts shade on the simple iron table and chairs and further height is provided by a trio of pencil cypress trees. Low, sinuous hedges of clipped rosemary and domes of *Teucrium fruticans* (tree germander) are planted in groups of three and cloud pruned into organic shapes. 'The idea is that in time they will fuse together.'

Accompanying many of the tightly clipped shrubs in the main garden are large cushions of Mexican fleabane (*Erigeron karvinskianus*). 'Erigeron is excellent for carpeting steps or gravel with its tiny daisy-like flowers in shades of white and pink.' Another useful perennial is *Oenothera lindheimeri*, AGM (gaura) which blooms profusely throughout the summer. 'Ultimately you want the garden to look good year-round. I aim for relaxed elegance without being too formal – instead of straight lines I prefer organic forms. I like to punctuate evergreens with flowers so that through the seasons you have moments of 'bang'.'

Even though the area benefits from a higher rainfall due to the encircling mountains, a drip line irrigation system has been installed. 'It's on a timer; we find that three times a week for 45 minutes is enough in summer,' he says.

The wildflower meadow below the garden terraces is left to its own devices. To marry the meadow with the formal garden, Alexander planted waves of soft grasses – *Stipa tenuissima* and pennisetum, alongside pale purple perovskia (now known as *Salvia* 'Blue Spire'), that merge seamlessly into the meadow. 'I like to blur the edges into the natural surroundings. I call it the transitional zone,' laughs Alexander.

Planted in spring 2023, the plants have romped away. 'It was a blank canvas and a challenging design, due to the different levels, but ultimately it was one of those projects that totally clicked.' ✤

■ mashambadesign.com

> "I aim for relaxed elegance without being too formal
> – instead of straight lines I prefer organic forms"

A mature olive tree and pencil cypress trees provide cool shade outside the main entrance of the house

A David Harber water feature offers a focal point on the small terrace at the back of the house

GARDEN GUIDE

Location Near the town of Puigpunyent, Mallorca, Balearic Islands, Spain.
Orientation and size Southwest facing, with landscaped areas of approx. 6,500sq m.
Soil type Soil varies from acidic clay in the lower parts of the garden to rocky soil in the higher areas.
Special features A formal garden with neat, clipped shrubs that gives way to ribbons of sinuous grasses and perennials that flow towards the wildflower meadow.
Garden designers Alexander and Jennifer Warren-Gash of Mashamba Garden Design.

An olive tree on top of
a stone wall overlooks a
path planted with neatly
clipped rosemary and
Teucrium fruticans
(tree germander)

Waves of purple
perovskia (*Salvia
'Blue Spire'*) and the
pale brown grass
Stipa tenuissima below
the main terrace

A canopy provides welcome shade on the dining terrace, which looks out to the fruit orchard beyond

Locally hewn stone steps connect the different garden levels

ZONING A GARDEN

■ I like to think of a garden as having different outdoor rooms, each with a theme. This gives your garden a purpose and invites you to spend more time outside.

■ One theme might be a sensory aromatic meadow, another might be a quiet spot with a hammock, hidden deep in the garden. It's these outdoor rooms that form part of the magic and charm of a well-designed garden.

■ Decide what you want from your outside space – a dining area, relaxing seating around a firepit, terraced pool area – all these are different zones. Once you have decided on your individual areas, you need to think about linking the spaces using a transitional planting scheme that carries you seamlessly from one to another.

■ Careful plant selection and placement creates a journey that's as stunning as the destination and invites you to take a relaxing stroll.

On the tiles

Tiling does wonders indoors and in the garden it
will add another layer of interest too

1.
Textural balance

The design of this small courtyard in Woollahra in
Sydney, Australia is warm and uplifting. Designer
Adam Robinson, working with Alexandra Kidd Interior
Design, explains: 'We had fun playing with the
horizontal and vertical lines of the bricks and tiles,
which are offset with sleek pavers and painted
wooden fencing. I love the contrast of the warmth
and character of the rustic brick wall with the
contemporary terracotta tile cladding, and then
the slick white fence – it's a great play on different
textures that create rhythm in the space. The design
exemplifies the warm face of minimalism – a modern
Mediterranean courtyard, embracing a pared-back
design aesthetic with a rustic, earthy colour palette.'

FEATURE JACKY HOBBS PHOTOGRAPH SUE STUBBS

2.
Mosaic marvel

The design and the materials chosen to illuminate and enliven this enclosed, previously gloomy London courtyard - as designer Lucy Sommers explains - were inspired by cascading water and a memory of Irish lagoons. Lucy inlaid a 'mosaic of blue-green river pebbles, their textural patterns resembling waves and ripples in the sand, in contrast to the more dynamic swirls of up-sided, foamy-white river pebbles' – which seemingly emanate from the shimmering stainless-steel water wall. Lucy worked with a specialist tile artist to create the 'convex, light-catching, shiny glazed clay bubble tiles' and it is these that elevate the look. 'Islands' of pooled echeveria and 'bankside' spheres of clipped evergreens anchor the innovative design.

3.
Playing with scale

Colour and geometry take centre stage in this tiled outdoor dining area. As interior and garden designer Emma Wood explains: 'The design was influenced by the client's love of pattern and print, with their garden an extension of their pattern-inspired interiors'. Emma choose a black hard-landscaped backdrop to allow the bold geometric tiles to highlight the social and eating spaces of the garden. 'Much as a painting creates a focal point in an interior,' says Emma, 'using tiles in complementary tones to create outdoor "rugs" or on features such as fireplaces adds distinctive highlights to an outdoor scheme. We treat garden design much as we would an interior space – flow, comfort and zoning still need to be maintained.' →

PHOTOGRAPHS (2) MARIANNE MAJERUS; (3) @JULIATOMSPHOTOGRAPHY

4.
Earth works

A key feature of this garden design inspired by forest bathing is the large, decorative bungaroosh-style wall, built using a mix of reclaimed and recycled materials: York stone blocks, slate, ridge tiles and bricks. Designer Ula Maria explains: 'I find reclaimed materials incredibly beautiful – rich in character, texture and patina. It is a shame we don't use them enough. This design is a celebration of reclaimed materials, showcasing how they can be used to create a beautiful and contemporary garden structure that's good for the environment and wildlife-friendly.' The 'green' backdrop settles harmoniously with Ula's woodland-style planting, including Siberian irises, grasses and Baltic parsley.

5.
Front runner

Senior designer Paul Robinson of AWB Associates explains how the stunning tiled floors to the porch and entrance lobby of a Victorian property inspired the garden design. This strong tradition of quality materials and attention to pattern, junctions and colour played an important part in the built elements of the space. 'The selected paving scheme offers a modern design update, which ingeniously honours the property's heritage and continues the use of premium materials to enhance the overall aesthetic,' he says. 'The materials chosen for this paving pattern include Ampilly limestone, crystal black granite with a bush-hammered finish and crystal black granite with a flamed finish. Planting in green, silver and cool hues completes the year-round muted tones of the garden.'

6.
Italian tapestry

An outdoor carpet of tiles brings a contemporary edge and pattern interest to an Italian courtyard garden centred around an ancient olive tree. Sunlight filters through the branches creating soft dappled shadows, which contrast with the repetitive geometry of the ceramic tiling — a recent outdoor addition to Italian brand Fioranese's Cementine tile collection (which can also be used to line swimming pools). 'The geometric design, Posa OpenAir 2, incorporates our hallmark light blue colouring,' says designer Silvia Stanzani, 'but comes in other colour solutions too, designed to be used as a single module or to complement the other five series patterns in the range.' →

7.
Creative contrast

Designer Stephen Woodhams has created an atmospheric rill garden with handcrafted tiles blurring the boundaries between colourful Marrakech and more muted Mallorca. 'Jade green glazed Moroccan zellige clay tiles enrich the design and work with the courtyard's green dribble-glazed pots,' says Stephen. 'Light bounces off the slightly uneven, highly reflective surface of the herringbone tile inlay, which frames the rill and accentuates the copper bowl feature.' The intricate tiling is stitched into a local landscaping material. The slabs are hewn from a nearby Mallorean quarry, Binissalem. 'Using locally sourced materials reduces the carbon footprint and supports local communities,' says Stephen.

8.
All natural

Designer Amelia Bouquet innovatively 'tiles' the vertical and horizontal spaces of this small garden with contrasting natural materials; stone, wood and living plants. Amelia explains that 'overlapping wooden "shingles" crafted by a Sussex carpenter using locally-grown, sustainable sweet chestnut and Douglas fir trees make up the decorative framed screen. They cast shadows, add texture and depth to the design and, layered in this ad hoc fashion, make a traditional tile seem more contemporary. In keeping are the sleek sandstone floor "planks", offset and interspersed with green fingers of creeping, shade-tolerant, ground-cover soleirolia. These mixed tiling techniques help create diversity, texture and contrast in a small scheme space, which denies a hard and fast divide between planting and landscaping.'

9.
Country seat

Designer and gardener Rachel Lamb reveals the origins of a curved, hand-painted, majolica-tile bench, nestling in the corner of an old Sicilian estate, where she collaborated (2002–2018) with the late owner Marchese Giuseppe Paternò Castello di San Giuliano. 'The seating, laid in the early 1990s, features old Sicilian blue-and-white tiles and a bust depicting the medieval king of Sicily, Federico II di Svevia. These were probably commissioned from Sicilian master ceramic artist, Giacomo Alessi. Wrapping around an old olive tree with typical Sicilian drystone wall at rear, the seating, designed by the marchese, was always a favourite spot, tucked away among fragrant and floriferous planting: *Pelargonium graveolens* in pots, climbing apricot roses and blue-eyed *Convolvulus sabatius*.'

PHOTOGRAPHS (8) JOANNA KOSSAK, RHS, HAMPTON COURT PALACE GARDEN FESTIVAL; (9) CLIVE NICHOLS

Solid hardwood floors

age beautifully over time

and last for generations.

Traditional oak, ash and elm floors sourced from well-managed British woodlands.

Expertly sawn and crafted in Wiltshire.

vastern.co.uk

Vastern Timber

Solid Hardwood Floors

The great outdoors

An edit of beautiful pieces for relaxing and entertaining in the sun

1.
2.
3.
4.
5.
6.
7.

Sitting comfortably

Armchairs you won't want to move from

1. Erica relax chair in Rust, from £3,721, Antonio Citterio for B&B Italia **2.** Grace chairs in Black, £1,799 each, Tove Kindt-Larsen for Gubi **3.** N3 Oak lounge chair in Pearl Herringbone, £865, Nth Degree **4.** Coast lounge chair with swivel in Umber Brown, £1,575, Cane-Line **5.** Settle lounge chairs in Laze 1 Grey, £1,499 each, Anderssen & Voll for Muuto at Royal Design **6.** Around deep seating armchair in Taupe Chalk, £1,440, Barlow Tyrie **7.** Ketch armchair in Merak 110 Burro, from £5,800, Jean-Marie Massaud for Poliform →

Sleek seats

Smart chairs for alfresco entertaining

Clement chair with cushion, £1,550, Rupert Bevan **2.** Chairs with buttoned cushions in standard Sunbrella fabric, £1,736.28 each, The Heveningham Collection **3.** Belmont dining side chair, £1,615, Munder Skiles **4.** RFH Terrace chair, £340, Robin Day for &Tradition at Twentytwentyone **5.** Palmer chair in Ochre/Toast with Ecru frame, €415, Honoré **6.** Sudbury dining chairs, £398 each; cushions in Navy Pinstripe, £98 each, all Rowen & Wren **7.** Palissade Cord dining chair in Iron Red, £439, Ronan Bouroullec for Hay at SCP

Top tables

Designs that feel at one with nature

1. Folding Coaching table, from £7,946, Howe **2.** Borge Mogensen M17 Ermelunden table, from £845, FDB Møbler at Utility Design **3.** Verdandi Garden dining table, £2,995, Oka **4.** Table 9A 120 in Teak with black base, from £835, Grythyttan Stålmöbler at SCP **5.** Wrought iron and teak garden table, £2,100, Susie Watson Designs **6.** Semley outdoor table, £1,555, Another Country **7.** Roller Max outdoor dining table, £1,729, Jacques Deneef for Ethnicraft →

Sun lounge

Sofas for relaxing in the heat

1. Osprey 3 seat sofa in Graphite and Gunmetal, £10,785, Janice Feldman for Janus et Cie **2.** Patio daybed, from £5,888, Studio Zanellato/Bortotto for Ethimo **3.** Longmeadow 2 seater sofa, £1,795, Neptune **4.** E520 with short backrest and side table, £2,208; E510 with backrest and armrest, £2,892, both EOOS Embrace Outdoor Lounge series, Carl Hansen & Søn. **5.** Akari lounge 3 seater sofa, £3,830, Vincent Sheppard **6.** Bordeaux 3 seater sofa, £1,699, Bridgman **7.** Burford 5 seater woven corner sofa, £1,499, John Lewis

Solid state

Durable tables for drinks and nibbles

1. Periscopio Arc Porphyry coffee table, £4,030, Studio Pepe for Exteta at Artemest **2.** Kenya coffee table, €3,500, Vittorio Paradiso for Paolo Castelli **3.** Pebble coffee table in Grey, £459, West Elm **4.** Lucca coffee table, £3,095, Andrew Martin **5.** Scalea table, from €3,742, Bernhardt & Vella for Arflex **6.** Matera low table in Palladiana Green, from £3,740, Paola Navone for Baxter at Monologue **7.** Cannelli coffee table in Brick, £549.99, La Redoute Interieurs 🔗

1.

2.

3.

4.

5.

6.

7.

Garden views

Ignacio Silva, National Trust head gardener at Emmetts Garden, tells us about the interesting plants to be found at one of the highest points in Kent

FEATURE HOLLY RANSOME PHOTOGRAPHS (PORTRAIT) NATIONAL TRUST IMAGES/MEGAN TAYLOR. (ROCK GARDEN) NATIONAL TRUST IMAGES/JOHN MILLER. © NATIONAL TRUST IMAGES, NATIONALTRUST.ORG.UK

"I'm from Galicia originally, where I grew up on a smallholding. I moved to the UK over 20 years ago and did my further gardening studies with the RHS and have been at Emmetts Garden near Sevenoaks for over three years now. The garden sprawls across six acres of a Site of Special Scientific Interest (SSSI) – due to the mixed woodland. We have beautiful views over the Kentish Weald and North Downs.

It used to be a farm but was bought in the late 1800s by Frederic Lubbock, a banker passionate about plants. The area was covered in giant anthills when he bought it – the word 'emmet' is an old colloquial word for ant.

The gardens, as we try to recapture them today, were influenced by Irish gardener William Robinson and planted with a mix of ornamental gardens, exotic trees and an Italian rose garden dedicated to Frederic's wife. There is a rare *Acer sinense*; a hundred-year-old handkerchief tree; and two Japanese maples, also about a hundred years old. My favourite is our Norway maple, closer to 150 years old.

Now that it's spring, the *Fritillaria meleagris*, *Narcissus* 'Hawera', rhododendrons and azaleas are all flowering. In the Rock Garden, the *Prunus incisa* 'Kojo-no-mai' is quite a sight and the orchard of *Prunus* 'Fugenzō' underplanted with tulips is about to look spectacular. In May, plants grow vigorously so it's important to keep on top of watering and make sure new growth has enough nutrients. We tend to our lawns and it's also a good time to sow seeds, remove weeds, edge beds and check for diseases. In the Rose Garden, we reseed the lawns with red fescue - it looks lovely and is low-maintenance.

Gardening requires lots of observing and trial and error – it's a job of patience and is weather-dependent. Results are not immediate and planning ideally should happen a year in advance. I would recommend keeping a diary with seasonal tasks and notes on how things develop. When introducing new plants, research their native location, preferred soil, moisture levels, aspect, pruning and feeding requirements, final height and spread, and possible pests and diseases to choose things that will thrive.

In my garden at home, I have many trees - it's like a small arboretum. The last thing I added was an *Agathis australis* tree. When I'm not at Emmetts or home, I visit other gardens for inspiration, like Stourhead in Wiltshire and Derek Jarman's garden in Dungeness."

Ignacio says gardening requires lots of observation

The Rock Garden in spring

TUMBLED AGED
Brass

A new bespoke finish.

Design Centre East, Chelsea Harbour
abiinteriors.co.uk

Kitchens & Bathrooms

SMART SOLUTIONS FOR THE BUSIEST SPACES

Chequerboard tiles take on a bold new character when extended up the walls of a shower space. Maroc porcelain tiles in Khaki and Beige, £89.38sq m, Ca' Pietra. Basin; taps; shower fittings, all Victrion range, BC Designs

Top designers discuss their dream schemes, statement showers, sociable kitchen islands and a selection of astute buys to consider

PROJECT NOTES

The latest launches and smart buys delivering luxury to kitchens and bathrooms

ABSOLUTE GEM

'A beautiful tap perfects a bathroom design in the same way that jewellery completes an outfit' is the mantra C.P. Hart's buying team live by, and Gessi's Inverso range certainly fulfils the brief. This single lever gem, with its woven metal handle and slim spout, will make a dreamy adornment to any wash area and it comes in this year's favourite chrome finish. Coordinate with matching bath mixers and shower controls, all available in 11 finishes. Gessi Inverso single lever basin mixer with Diamantato handle in Chrome, from £399, C.P. Hart.

TALL ORDER

Thoughtful design meets artisanal craftsmanship in this new partner to Neptune's Tilbury dining chair. The Tilbury bar stool, £495, blends the warmth of oak with the charm of woven rattan. Built with traditional mortise and tenon joints for durability, the frame is sealed with IsoGuard to help protect it, while the rattan-webbed seat has just enough flex to ensure proper comfort.

SOAK IT IN

Inspired by the art of traditional Japanese bathing, the Onsen bath by Adamsez combines compact elegance with indulgent relaxation. Designed for a deep soak, its plunge-style depth and integrated internal bench ensure a comfortable experience. The bath is available in any RAL shade through the AdColour service. Onsen bath, £2,067; optional step, £205, Adamsez.

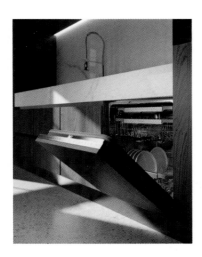

CLEAN UP

If you're in the market for a new dishwasher, put Signature Kitchen Suite's Quadwash at the top of your list. This integrated model sprays jets of water in four directions to ensure sparkling clean dishes every time. The option of steam injection for stubborn deposits and a super-quiet direct drive motor make this a game-changer for kitchens. Signature Kitchen Suite SKSDW2402P Quadwash dishwasher, £2,100, Falmec.

Bold statement

Rangemaster has reimagined its Elise Luxe range cooker with a sleek new facelift. The new Elise Luxe Black Edition elevates classic French-inspired styling with modern cruciform controls, handles and trim in Jet Black and Antique Brass, perfectly aligning with the trend for dark kitchen accents. Priced from £4,699, this striking cooker is available in induction (pictured) or dual-fuel models. 🖼

GATHER ROUND

From breakfast bars to banquettes, island units with seating have great influence on how we come together in the kitchen

SOLID CHOICE

Few things rival the impact of a chunky cantilevered stone slab when it comes to creating a standout seating area on your island. In this project, Cabbonet went all in with dramatically veined Arabescato Orobico marble in swirling rust and grey tones. 'Visually, this cantilevered seating area brings a sense of modern elegance, enhancing the open, airy feel of the room by eliminating the need for support legs. This not only frees up floor space but also creates a more expansive atmosphere,' explains Andrew Hays, founder and creative director, Cabbonet. 'It's a versatile spot for casual dining, prepping or entertaining,' adds Andrew.

Bespoke kitchen in brass, oak and marble, from £50,000, Cabbonet. Mater high stools by Space Copenhagen, £864 each, Viaduct

FEATURE LINDA CLAYTON PHOTOGRAPH GEORGE SHARMAN

TABLE TALK

So, you've set your heart on a banquette, now let's talk tables. 'A lightweight table that can be easily moved closer or further from the banquette ensures comfort,' says Reuben Ward, lead designer at Blakes London. Reuben also recommends avoiding tables with legs at the ends, as they can make sliding in and out of the banquette tricky. 'Pedestal tables are ideal.' **Standard Dakota table base in brass, £3,935, Julian Chichester. Bespoke kitchen in stained oak and Macaubas quartzite, from £55,000, Blakes London**

IN GOOD SHAPE

An L-shaped dining set-up on a kitchen island brings more to the table than a simple row of stools ever could, so says Charlie Smallbone, founder of Ledbury Studio. 'They provide a more intimate and sociable seating arrangement, allowing diners to face each other rather than all sitting in a row,' he says. 'This layout encourages better conversation flow and creates a cosy dining atmosphere.' **Leather strap bar stools in Tan, £390 each, Six The Residence. Bespoke kitchen, from £70,000, Ledbury Studio →**

PHOTOGRAPHS (TABLE TALK) MALCOLM MENZIES @82MMPHOTOGRAPHY

MIDDLE GROUND

Placing a dining area between two islands requires a generous footprint, but when you have the luxury of space to indulge, it creates a layout that's as striking as it is versatile. 'The seating area here is large enough that you can easily fit 10 people if you pull chairs up, but cosy enough that it could be just two people enjoying a meal,' says Emma Deterding, founder of Kelling Designs.

A similar deVOL kitchen with Corian worktops and leather banquette seating would start at £85,000 at Kelling Designs

MAKE IT PERSONAL

A banquette is a chance to add colour and pattern to your kitchen. This vibrant space by Own London features fun stripes and Aztec prints for a burst of energy. 'One of the beauties of banquettes is that they can be tailored to match various styles, from rustic farmhouse charm to sleek, modern aesthetic,' says Alicia Meireles, creative director at Own London.

Banquette in Plain Stripe glazed cotton in Ruby, £154m, Flora Soames. Dining chairs in Nomad linen in Teal by Mulberry Home, £149m, GP & J Baker. Bespoke kitchen by Own London

PHOTOGRAPHS (MIDDLE GROUND) PAUL MASSEY. (MAKE IT PERSONAL) DARREN CHUNG FOR ONE MENAGERIE

PULL UP A STOOL

When your island takes centre stage upon entering the room, it's essential to choose good-looking stools. Venetia Rudebeck, co-founder of Studio Vero, aced the brief with these bronze stools by Rose Uniacke. 'Our client loves entertaining, so the island had to be both a statement piece and functional for everyday use,' says Venetia, noting the stools have deep padded seats and lumbar support that make them exceptionally comfortable. Upholstered bar stools with back rest, from £1,620 each, Rose Uniacke. Cabinets in Middle Buff intelligent eggshell, £80 for 2.5ltr, Little Greene. Linoleum floor tiles, £95.50sq m, Sinclair Till. Hanley Tube Lined wall tiles, £1,969.38sq m, Balineum. Bespoke fluted island, around £20,000, Studio Vero →

LOW PROFILE

A drop-level, table-style dining area on your island is a game-changer for functionality and style. 'By lowering part of the island to standard dining table height, you create a versatile space that bridges the gap between casual and formal dining,' says Jayne Everett, creative designer, Naked Kitchens. Sitting at regular dining chairs is also a more ergonomic option, catering to guests who may find bar stools less inviting.

Houghton kitchen in walnut and Lavender Fields, from £25,000, Naked Kitchens

DO THE MATHS

Island seating can serve as a quick perch for coffee or wine, but if you plan to linger, comfort is key. Interior designer Bethany Adams appreciates the importance of measurements. 'For counter seating, knee depth is just as crucial as clearance height. As table height increases, the required knee space decreases – 46cm for a table, 38cm for a counter-height island and just 30cm for a bar-height island,' she says.

A similar custom kitchen by Bethany Adams Interiors would start at £123,000. Chubby counter stools, £1,080 each, Dirk van der Kooij

PHOTOGRAPHS (DO THE MATHS) J.L. JORDAN

Distracting, by design

Art Select.
Always stealing the moment

DESIGNER KITCHEN

Interior designer Adam Bray's dream scheme eschews fitted cabinetry and champions individual elements instead

BEAUTY WITH UTILITY

Adam Bray is known for his expert eye for antique furniture, textiles and unusual objects, coupled with an ability to transform interiors with a sophisticated use of colour (he has designed two collections of cabinet colours for Plain English). 'I like kitchens to feel as if they are made from elements, rather than completely fitted,' he says. Preferred options might include a free-standing vitrine, a vintage dining table and an antique cupboard. 'They bring in the patina of age, which blends so well with modern utilitarian pieces, such as a large La Cornue range or industrial ovens from Wolf,' he adds. 'While I enjoy both strong and faded colours, the choice will depend on the setting, and I do think our wallpaper collection from Hamilton Weston looks really great and fresh in a traditional kitchen.'

1. **PD9 Modern Day refectory table**, £13,800, Patch Rogers
2. **Mercier vitrine in black stained oak with glass**, £23,600, Pinch
3. **Blanc Antique enamelled lava stone worktop**, from £1,500sq m, Pyrolave
4. **DCWéditions Lampe Gras 304L wall light**, £357, Twentytwentyone
5. **Zanotta April folding armchair by Gae Aulenti**, £1,487, Chaplins
6. *The Zuni Café Cookbook by Judy Rodgers* (£28.99, W.W. Norton & Company)
7. **Brown Paper Stripe wallpaper in Blue**, £195.60 for a 10m roll, Adam Bray for Hamilton Weston Wallpapers
8. **ICBDF60650CG/S/P range cooker**, £32,880, Wolf

FEATURE AMELIA THORPE PHOTOGRAPHS (2) JAMES MERRELL

SHOWERING PRAISE

These statement designs deserve top marks
for the way they bring beauty and character
to the most practical room in the house

1.

CONTAIN YOURSELF

For a statement shower that doubles as a luxurious piece of furniture, look no further than Drummonds' self-contained Thurso shower. Featuring an all-glass surround and unlacquered brass finish that will patina with age, this stunning piece allows beautiful wallpaper and artwork to be fully enjoyed, while allowing natural light to flow freely through the space. 'As a fully enclosed unit, it offers complete freedom of placement and ensures a seamless integration with your interior,' says James Lentaigne, managing director of Drummonds. 'This level of flexibility is incredibly useful, especially in older properties where altering walls for a shower enclosure invariably diminishes the room's original character.' With its 360° views, the experience inside is just as captivating as the one outside.

The Thurso freestanding shower in Unlacquered Brass, £32,988, Drummonds

FEATURE LINDA CLAYTON PHOTOGRAPH OLI DOUGLAS

2.

LEVEL UP

Accessibility was the driving force behind the creation of this walk-in shower, but its execution was all about refined aesthetic details. For the owners of this 2005 Craftsman home in Virginia, level access was a practical necessity, but they envisioned it being delivered with sophistication. Enter Tanya Smith-Shiflett of Unique Kitchens and Baths, who collaborated with Sara Swabb of Storie Collective on this dreamy shower. 'The project prioritised cohesive material selections and intentional design,' Tanya says. 'For instance, the elegant archway with moulded marble trim beautifully frames the entrance, while the stone floor, laid in a chequered pattern, flows seamlessly into the shower, creating both visual interest and a sense of movement.'

BC Designs' Senator bath, from £4,198, is similar. Project by Storie Collective and Unique Kitchens and Baths

3.

HEAD TO TOE

Enjoy an indulgent, spa-like experience with a shower featuring body jets – few do it with more flair than Catchpole & Rye's handmade La Cage. This piece delivers a fully immersive showering experience with a 12" overhead shower rose and more than 200 jets. 'When selecting an enclosure like our La Cage, it is essential to consider space and height requirements. It's not just about fitting it physically but ensuring it works beautifully as a feature in the room,' says head of design, Lizzi Catchpole. The aged brass finish here contrasts beautifully with the vibrant tiles, turning this shower into a true statement piece. 'Stepping inside is a wonderfully immersive experience, like truly having your own in-home spa,' adds Lizzi.

La Cage shower, £20,160; The Original Ladder towel rail, £3,456, both in Aged Brass, Catchpole & Rye →

PHOTOGRAPHS (2) STACY ZARIN GOLDBERG

4.

DRAW A LINE

Challenging shower spaces often inspire some of the most creative design solutions. This clever use of mosaic tiles in a shower tucked into the eaves of a Paris loft bathroom proves that even the most awkward spaces can impress. By employing Bisazza's joyful pinstripe pink mosaics, Mother & Daughter Interior has cleverly ironed out many of the angles, transforming a tricky layout into a striking feature.

'Mosaics are ideal for maximising challenging spaces, offering seamless coverage and effortlessly navigating curves and corners without drawing attention to structural imperfections,' explains Donna Podger, national sales manager at Bisazza London.

Pinstripe Pink glass mosaics from the Opus Romano Collection by India Mahdavi, from £370sq m, Bisazza. Project by Mother & Daughter Interior

5.

LOUNGE STYLE

'For a luxurious shower experience, give yourself as much space as possible so that you feel like you are in a five-star hotel,' says Louise Ashdown, head of design at West One Bathrooms. 'Features like built-in seating, rainfall shower heads and steam generators provide all the incentives you need to linger longer and embrace the wellness benefits.' This indulgent theme can extend beyond the shower with a lounge area, which Louise notes is becoming increasingly popular. 'To maximise the sense of openness, choose pale colours – avoiding stark white – and add texture through tiles,' she adds.

Thermostatic valve, £3,090; volume control handles, £1,476 each; hand shower and hose, £1,084; shower head, £3,133, all in Unlacquered Brass, Pinna Paletta collection by Kallista; similar shower screen in polished brass, £2,051, all West One Bathrooms

PHOTOGRAPH INGRID RASMUSSEN

6.

MATERIAL WORLD

In this striking space by interior designer Verity Woolf, the fusion of materials seamlessly blends the cool elegance of lava stone countertops with the smooth sophistication of natural marble, the subtle grain of walnut and the velvety touch of microcement. 'The organic swirls of blue marble in the shower provide a dramatic contrast to the vibrant, 70s-inspired Formica and acrylic finishes,' says Verity. 'Each material invites touch, making the room both a visual and deeply tactile experience.'

Bespoke walnut mirror cabinet, £21,640; lacquered vanity unit carcass with walnut and brass trim, £15,060, Rupert Bevan. Blue Jupiter chandelier, £1,010, Juanma Lizana Studio. Terrazzo 07 floor tiles, from £96sq m, Archi Tile. Cullifords stocks similar Calcite Blue marble, £990sq m. Project by Woolf Interior Architecture & Design →

7.

PERFECT PARTNERS

Gather your shower and bath into one wet-room-style arrangement for the ultimate luxe-meets-functional scheme. This semi open-plan layout by ABI Interiors oozes contemporary sophistication while maximising space, but nailing the practical details was vital. 'We recommend including a separate hand-shower to make it easier to rinse the bath after showering. A slim glass screen is also handy for keeping vanity areas dry,' says Renee Enoka, interior designer, ABI Interiors. Top it off with a statement skylight – flooding the space with natural light for invigorating morning showers and calming twilight soaks.

Shower head and mount, £187.98; gooseneck hob swivel basin tap spout, £102.99; Milani hob mixer controls, £134.99; 3-function round hand shower, £69.99, all in Brushed Copper; Zuri undercounter basin, £181.99, ABI Interiors

8.

MARBLE MOMENT

Embrace the beauty of solid marble slabs, expertly cut for minimal joints and effortless drainage. 'Bringing a unique piece of nature into your bathroom will infuse your space with warmth and personality,' says Lisa Persse, director of Porter Bathroom, who orchestrated this striking walk-in marble shower for interior designer Laura Butler-Madden. 'The slab design reduces grout lines, making it a seamless, easy-to-maintain shower.'

Hepworth shower diverter, £966; Pelham shower head, £444; hand hose, £394.20; Hepworth large floor towel rail, £1,638; ribbed shower screen with fixed arm, £2,340; bespoke shower tray in Calacatta Rosa Antica marble, price on request, Porter Bathroom. Mineral N3 Herringbone wood flooring, £138sq m, Trunk Floor. Walls in Holland Park No.5 marble matt emulsion, £64.50 for 2.5ltr, Mylands ◨

PHOTOGRAPHS (8) PATRICK BUTLER-MADDEN

DESIGNER BATHROOM

A luxurious aesthetic that awakens the senses is interior designer Joanna Plant's idea of a dream bathing space

HEIGHT OF ELEGANCE

'The showstopper of my dream bathroom is a marble tub, filled to the brim with scented hot water to enjoy while reading a book,' says interior designer Joanna Plant. Known for comfortable rooms that celebrate colour and a sense of timeless elegance, Joanna would set the bath against walls painted in Edward Bulmer's Lilac Pink, sumptuously interlined curtains made up in Bennison Fabrics' Songbird linen and a vanity in dramatic Breche Violette marble. 'Above the vanity, I'd hang a Venetian mirror with antique Baguès wall lights to add a little sparkle and a whole lot of glamour,' she says. A slipper chair to throw clothes on, nickel taps and beautiful monogrammed bath linens are also part of the chic scheme. 'Keeping splashes to a minimum, I'd have rush matting on the floor as I loathe the coldness of tiles underfoot and rush lends a wonderful texture and delicious scent,' she notes.

1. **Dolly country-style dish**, £88, Astier de Villatte
2. **19th century French armoire**, £3,650, Maison Artefact
3. **Songbird linen** in Pink Green on Oyster, £350m, Bennison Fabrics
4. **The Single Lowther vanity basin**, from £4,926, Drummonds
5. **The Mull Classic Bridge mixer tap** in Polished Nickel, £1,356, Drummonds
6. **Melograno bath salts**, £41, Santa Maria Novella
7. **Lilac Pink emulsion**, £66 for 2.5ltr, Edward Bulmer Natural Paint
8. **Italian Roman Moleanos limestone bath**, from £29,940, Lapicida

FEATURE AMELIA THORPE

Lifestyle

FOOD, TRAVEL AND OTHER WONDERFUL THINGS

This delightful space is designer Beata Heuman's kitchen in her home in Sweden. We talk to her on page 186.
Snowdrop rise and fall light, Beata Heuman

&

We're following the sun with an insider's guide to Portugal's beguiling beachside villages and Italian dishes that feel like sunshine on a plate, plus designer Beata Heuman reveals her loves

171

A LOVE LETTER TO...

Interior designer Alexandra Champalimaud explains why a certain
stretch of Portuguese coastline holds a special place in her heart

FEATURE EMMA J PAGE PHOTOGRAPHS (VERMELHO) ©AMBROISE TÉZENAS

COMPORTA has been a destination for me and my family for years. As well as its namesake, the area is home to a number of small villages, most just over an hour south of Lisbon. They hug a 75 kilometre stretch of wild Atlantic beach – in my opinion, the best in Europe. Exuding the charm and authenticity of the agricultural Portuguese Alentejo countryside, the region remains real and is all the more beguiling for it.

■ I spend my days exploring wide sandy beaches or walking through wildflowers under magnificent cork trees in the countryside. Comporta and the surrounding area is ideal for long lunches at the beach, enjoying local seafood and spending leisurely time with friends old and new.

■ We always make a beeline for our favourite restaurants: Cavalariça (top left) serves classic dishes in a rustic family style from a converted stable. Meanwhile, in a charming old building,

Mesa is unpretentious and serves local dishes like seabass ceviche. And at Gomes, we enjoy the oysters and a broad selection of wines.

■ There are a number of small beach villages just south of Comporta, including Carvalhal. There, Deli Comporta, a recent addition, has quickly become a favourite of mine. The food is respectful of local tradition, the decor is cosmopolitan and the vibe gets lively as the evening wears on.

■ A long-time favourite, now relocated at Praia do Carvalhal, Sal has a distinct mood and is beloved by many. The food is moreish. I can never pass up Amêijoas à Bulhão Pato (simply cooked small clams) and whichever freshly caught whole fish is on offer that day, washed

down with a glass of local wine. Next door, the Sublime Beach Club is the perfect spot for whiling away an entire day.

■ When it comes to unearthing special pieces, I often get the most enjoyment from Feiras, the local roadside markets that pop up between villages. I have found treasured items there, like hand-painted bowls made by local potters.

■ Melides, another small beach village to the south, is a favourite. Stay at Christian Louboutin's hotel Vermelho (top right), a reconstruction of a centuries-old convent. It's a study in the style of its creator, filled with colour. There, I also like to head to Noemina, a highly personal shop owned by Noemi Cinzano featuring clothing, linens and accessories.

> "I spend my days exploring wide sandy beaches or walking through wildflowers in the countryside"

LA DOLCE VITA

These Italian regional recipes will transport
you to the sun-drenched villages that line
the glittering Tyrrhenian Sea

VERY THIN COURGETTE AND BASIL OMELETTE

SERVES 1 AS A MAIN OR 2-3 AS A STARTER
2 organic eggs
Sea salt and freshly ground black pepper
25g unsalted butter
1 tbsp olive oil
1 courgette (about 150g),
sliced into thin discs
Handful of basil leaves, roughly torn
20g Parmesan, finely grated

- Crack the eggs into a bowl, add a generous pinch of salt and a few grinds of pepper and whisk with a fork.

- Melt the butter with the olive oil in a wide frying pan over a medium heat. Pick up the pan and swirl the fat around so that it goes up the side of the pan to avoid the egg sticking later. Once it starts to sizzle, add the courgette and gently toss to ensure it is evenly coated. Leave to cook without stirring for 3-4 minutes. Add the basil and toss, turning all the courgette slices over. Cook for another 3-4 minutes until the slices are golden and the basil has wilted.

- Make sure the courgette is evenly spaced in one layer over the base of the pan. Pour over the beaten egg, then gently swirl the pan to allow it to evenly coat the courgette. Cook without stirring for 2-3 minutes. Once the egg starts to look opaque at the bottom, sprinkle over the grated Parmesan, then leave for another minute or so until the bottom is completely cooked, the top is set and the cheese has melted.

- Using a spatula, gently ease onto a serving plate. Top with freshly ground pepper and serve immediately. →

LINGUINE WITH ANCHOVY, BREADCRUMBS AND LEMON ZEST

SERVES 4

40g fine breadcrumbs
25 good-quality anchovy fillets preserved in oil
4 garlic cloves, crushed
100ml olive oil
Sea salt
400g linguine
Grated zest of 2 lemons
Handful of flat-leaf parsley, roughly chopped

▪ Toast the breadcrumbs in a small frying pan over a medium heat for 3 minutes or until golden brown. Transfer to a bowl and set aside.

▪ Tip the anchovy fillets and their oil into a small bowl and stir in the garlic. Add to a frying pan large enough to toss all the cooked pasta, along with half the olive oil. Reduce the heat to low and gently heat for 3-5 minutes, allowing the anchovy fillets to melt and disintegrate into the warm oil. Add the rest of the oil and continue to infuse, being careful not to let it burn.

▪ Meanwhile, bring a large saucepan of salted water to the boil. Add the linguine, give it a good stir so that it doesn't stick together, and cook until al dente (about 9 minutes, but check the packet instructions). Halfway through the cooking time, add half a ladleful of the starchy pasta water to the anchovy oil and let it bubble and amalgamate while the pasta cooks.

▪ Using tongs, transfer the pasta to the frying pan and toss through the anchovy oil, then add the lemon zest. Divide the pasta among four bowls, sprinkle with the chopped parsley and finish with a sprinkling of the golden breadcrumbs.

SEA BASS WITH PISTACHIOS, PINE NUTS AND SUN-DRIED TOMATOES

SERVES 4
50g unsalted pistachios
2 tbsp olive oil, plus extra for brushing and drizzling
4 large sea bass fillets, pin-boned
Sea salt and freshly ground black pepper
6 large sun-dried tomatoes in oil, drained and finely chopped
2 tbsp pine nuts

- Preheat the oven to 200°C/Gas 6.

- Blitz the pistachios in a food processor to a chunky, coarse consistency. Set aside in a small bowl.

- Line a roasting tin with baking parchment and brush with a little olive oil so the fish won't stick. Add the fish fillets, skin side down, and season with salt and pepper. Evenly sprinkle a heaped teaspoon of the ground pistachios over each fillet and top with a teaspoon of sun-dried tomatoes, a few pine nuts, a little salt and pepper and a drizzle of olive oil.

- Bake for 10-11 minutes or until the fish is white and flaky. Remove from the oven and serve immediately. →

RASPBERRY TIRAMISU

SERVES 6
650g raspberries, rinsed
Juice of ½ lemon
100ml sweet marsala wine
75g caster sugar
4 organic egg yolks
500g mascarpone
3 organic egg whites
About 24 savoiardi (ladyfinger biscuits)

■ This is how to make one large tiramisu, but you can make individual ones if you prefer. Start by roughly slicing the raspberries in half. Place in a bowl and cover with the lemon juice, wine and 1 tablespoon of sugar. Cover and set aside at room temperature for an hour or up to overnight in the fridge.

■ Using handheld electric beaters, whisk the egg yolks with the remaining sugar for 2-3 minutes. Whisk in the mascarpone and set aside. In a clean metal bowl and with clean beaters, whisk the egg whites to soft peaks. Fold the egg whites into the mascarpone mixture.

■ Tip the raspberries into a small colander over a bowl to separate the liquid from the pulp (the bowl should be large enough to dip the biscuits into). Set aside the pulp.

■ Half dip the biscuits, sugar side down, into the liquid. Cover the bottom of your serving dish with a layer of dipped biscuits, sugar side up, then spoon over a third of the pulp. Spoon over half the mascarpone cream, smoothing it out with a spatula or the back of a spoon. Repeat with another layer of dipped ladyfingers, half the remaining the pulp and the rest of the mascarpone cream. Mix together the remaining pulp and soaking liquid and spoon over the top.

■ Cover and leave in the fridge for at least 4 hours; remove from the fridge 30 minutes before serving.

PROSECCO, LIMONCELLO AND BASIL COCKTAIL

SERVES 6
Ice cubes, to serve
Handful of basil leaves
90ml homemade or shop-bought limoncello
1 bottle good-quality dry Prosecco
Soda water, to taste
6 lemon slices

■ Fill a glass with plenty of ice and a few basil leaves. Pour over 15ml limoncello, followed by about 125ml Prosecco and a splash of soda water. Gently stir to combine. Add a slice of lemon to the glass and garnish with a few more basil leaves. Repeat to make five more (or increase quantities to make as many as you like). ■

Extracted from
ITALIAN COASTAL: RECIPES AND STORIES FROM WHERE THE LAND MEETS THE SEA
by Amber Guinness
(£29.99, Thames & Hudson Australia)

A GREAT ESCAPE

Set across five heritage buildings, The Largo offers a unique and creative connection to Porto and its people

NESTLED behind a large, unmarked green door in the bustling historic square of Largo de São Domingos lies The Largo, a beautiful 18-room boutique hotel that champions community, connection and innovation. Portuguese architect Frederico Valsassina and Danish design studio Space Copenhagen are behind the restoration and serene design of this elevated private residence, led by Danish travel and hospitality collective, Annassurra.

The contemporary and minimalist design of The Largo embodies all that we have come to know and love about the understated 'quiet luxury' look. The generously sized rooms and suites are defined by an interplay of soft, organic colour palettes and a luxurious use of natural materials. Moments of alluring contrast are created throughout the hotel by the installation of many modern artworks, including Rui Chafes' eldritch steel sculpture, *Luz Sobriamente Pura*, which greets you as you ascend the stairs to Terraço; the rooftop lounge and kitchen with views over the city.

The Largo prides itself on a deeply rooted connection to Porto and its people – and this could not be more evident than through its exquisite offering of food and drink. Adjoined to The Largo is Flôr, a contemporary cocktail bar where experimental concoctions take centre stage, and Cozinha das Flores, a restaurant headed by acclaimed Lisbon-born chef, Nuno Mendes – the savoury pastel de nata with turnip and caviar was utterly divine. Not to mention the impressive hidden wine cellar.

For those wanting to enhance their stay further, three times a year, The Largo hosts a *Porto Unknown* package, which honours Northern Portugal's rich traditions through a series of curated seasonal events. Remaining celebrations at the hotel this year are taking place in June and October, centring around Porto's maritime and gastronomic heritage. From culinary workshops to coastal foraging excursions, you can look forward to an immersive fusion of cultural exploration and luxurious hospitality. 🖼

"The contemporary and minimalist design embodies all that we have come to know and love about the understated 'quiet luxury' look"

FEATURE ZARA STACEY

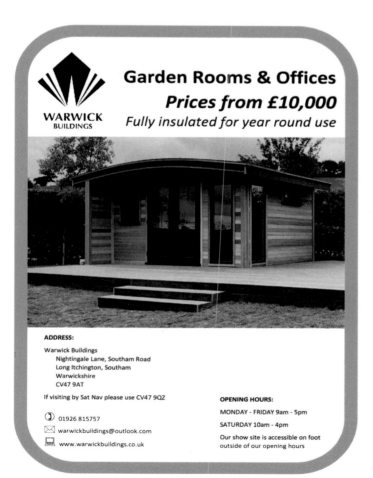

MY LIFE IN 10

Beata Heuman, interior designer and maker of homeware and furnishings, shares some of her favourite things

1. Reading is a huge part of my life. When I studied literature at university I jotted down specific quotes that resonated to inspire me when writing my essays and I still do that. Returning to these notes is to revisit the essence of a book. One book I often return to is *Against Design* by Josef Frank.

2. My parents would never take me on a beach holiday but they would drive me and my three siblings from Sweden to Normandy to show us the Bayeux Tapestry. It is not what I wanted but it has stood me in good stead. Art has the ability to make you see things through someone else's eyes and the more you see, the more it opens your mind.

3. A long soak in Wiberg's Pine Bath Essence reminds me of when I first moved to England, of rainy walks and flush cheeks and anticipation of what might happen that evening.

4. My studio, an 1820s building at 188 Hammersmith Road, is my epicentre. It's a canvas to experiment, a home environment into which we can invite clients and customers and friends but, best of all, a wonderful place for us all to work, learn and get inspired.

5. We go to our house in the south of Sweden when the girls have a longer break from school. I thrive off the energy, possibilities and people in London but it is healthy and refreshing to get a different perspective.

6. A recent addition: my La Marzocco Linea Micra coffee machine makes me get up in the morning. I enjoy the ritual, the smell, the frothy milk - the whole shebang!

7. I could never get bored of Florence, the restaurants such as Cammillo and Sergio Gozzi and Negroni Sbagliatos in Rivoire and shopping at Loretta Caponi.

8. Cooking is my way of winding down and relaxing while still doing something useful. My friend Amber Guinness' cookbook *A House Party in Tuscany* has been a huge inspiration and my new favourite is *The Farm Table* by my friend and brilliant collaborator Julius Roberts.

9. There is nothing quite like slipping into a freshly made bed with crisp, ironed sheets. A comfortable bed is a joy forever – and a big reason to design a collaboration with Mille Notti.

10. I listen to podcasts whenever I can: doing the laundry, cooking, exercising (although if I'm doing a run I may change *The Rest is History* to some Tinie Tempah to get myself into sprint mode).

From top, clockwise Beata Heuman has childhood memories of visits to see the Bayeux Tapestry in France; she loves a long soak in Wiberg's Pine Bath Essence and is a big fan of podcasts

FEATURE JESSICA SALTER **PHOTOGRAPHS** (PORTRAIT) SOPHIE DAVIDSON; (BAYEUX TAPESTRY) © BAYEUX MUSEUM